**BEANO AND THE DANDY
CLASSIC COMIC COVERS
1937-1988**

First published September 2019 by:

phil-comics
Vintage comic dealers and auctioneers
35 Brook Road, Bassingbourn, Hertfordshire, SG8 5NR

www.phil-comics.com

A Beano Studios Product © DC Thomson Ltd. (2019)
Licensed by Rocket Licensing Ltd.

Concept and layout of this book, along with the text, by Phil Shrimpton.

phil-comics gratefully acknowledges Angeles Blanco, Amy Pearson and Usha Chauhan of Beano Studios Ltd. and Joanne Davey of Rocket Licensing Ltd. in the licensing of material from *Beano* and *The Dandy*.

A big thank-you to Hilary Mudie of Download Media Ltd. for reprographic and graphic design work.

Many thanks to Leah Grant for copyediting and proofreading the text.

Whilst a number of comic covers in this book originated from the personal collection of the publisher, Phil Shrimpton, several private collectors very kindly contributed covers from their own collections. Our sincere thanks go to Stuart Jay, Simon Kidd, Chris Sendall, David Jones, Adam Teitge, Barry Reynolds and Darren Collett for supplying scans to be included in this book.

A thank-you to Duncan Laird of the Archive Department, DC Thomson & Co., Ltd., for supplying scans of the original artwork for front covers featured. They are *Beano* No. 861, 911, 1640 and *The Dandy* No. 2249.

A special thank-you to Liz Shrimpton for her love and support.

Some pages may contain references which are of their time but would not be considered suitable today. The following *Beano* covers have had the racial stereotype character Peanut removed and *The Beano Comic* logo and associated text moved to a central position: Issue No. 1, 15, 26, 47, 49, 101, 120, 168, 169, 170, 177, 195 and 247. All other covers appear exactly as they were originally published.

All rights reserved. This book is sold subject to the condition that it may not be reproduced, stored in a retrieval system or transmitted in any form or by any means, electronic, mechanical, photocopying, recording or otherwise, without the prior consent of the publisher and copyright holders.

A catalogue record for this book is available from the British Library.

Printed and bound in Malta by Gutenberg Press Ltd.

Printed on FSC-accredited paper.

ISBN 978-0-9926635-1-3

2 4 6 8 10 9 7 5 3 1

phil-comics

**For Alfred**

# KEEP AN EYE ON "THE BEANO" EVERY THURSDAY

*Beano* and *The Dandy* need little introduction. Adored by millions of children spanning multiple generations, these two popular comics have – over the past eighty years – poked fun at authority, provided endless laughs, created well-known, beloved characters and reached national treasure status.

Current readers of *Beano* have recently enjoyed its 4,000th issue, published in August 2019. Officially the world's longest running weekly comic, *Beano* celebrated its 80th birthday in July last year and remains in fine form today with a growing weekly readership.

*The Dandy*, by contrast, ceased publication as a weekly comic in December 2012, coinciding with its 75th birthday, but it is fondly remembered by fans, and its legacy is still enjoyed with various specials and an annual published each year at Christmas.

This new collection of comic covers follows on from our first book, published in 2013 and featuring the wonderful Christmas covers of *Beano* and *The Dandy* from 1937 to 1969.

It was a pleasure to bring so many scarcely seen, festive covers together in that first book, and this latest collection – which celebrates some of the very best covers from the first fifty years of *Beano* and *The Dandy* – offers a similar opportunity to explore a variety of rare and familiar covers, this time across five glorious decades.

Eighty covers of each comic have been chosen, spanning 1937 to 1988. We thought it fitting to start with the No. 1 issues of each comic and end with the 50th birthday issues, No. 2402. The process of selecting the remaining covers was no mean feat; indeed, how does one go about whittling down such a vast and generous archive to just eighty covers of each title?

In order to understand the selection process, it is vital that we first consider the history of *Beano* and *The Dandy*, the importance of eye-catching covers and the creation of characters who are as celebrated as the comics themselves.

Produced on the same floor in the DC Thomson & Co., Ltd. headquarters in Dundee, *Beano* and *The Dandy* started life just a few short months apart in the late 1930s. Back then, front covers were a major selling point for weekly readers. Many comics were competing for attention at the newsagent, so each cover had to be brighter, bolder and more appealing than its rivals. To retain loyal youngsters and garner new readership, a popular cover star was required.

Big Eggo appeared on the cover of the first issue of *Beano* in 1938. Drawn by Reg Carter, the zany ostrich held this spot for 326 issues. Excerpts from *Beano: 80 Years of Fun* offer a fascinating insight into the character creation of Big Eggo: it was suggested to artist Reg Carter that when drawing Eggo he should draw a very human bird and "play up to all the characteristics of an ostrich – eat anything, hide its head in the sand, kick like a mule, run fast" and to be "always looking for an egg he has lost." Furthermore, the artist "could afford to be almost ludicrous, with big feet and big goggled eyes and plenty of exaggerated expression." Carter's work did not disappoint, and Big Eggo enjoyed a decade of eccentric exploits on the cover.

In 1948, fur replaced feathers when Biffo the Bear burst onto the scene with issue No. 327. Biffo was a rather calamitous bear at times but was also a gentle, fun-loving character who had everyone's best interests at heart. Biffo was created by one of DC Thomson & Co., Ltd.'s greatest comic artists, Dudley Watkins, who drew the friendly bear until late 1969 when he died at his easel whilst halfway through a Biffo strip. After Watkins passed away, David Sutherland took over the drawing of Biffo with great skill.

# WHIZZ BANG FIREWORKS NUMBER

Appearing from 1951 and drawn by David Law, Dennis is the most famous character from *Beano*. In 1970, David Sutherland took over the strip, and in No. 1678, September 1974, Dennis and Gnasher burst onto the front cover spot where they have remained almost exclusively to this day. The duo remain loveable rogues who have entertained generations of readers.

The first issue of *The Dandy*, published in late 1937, featured the comic's most famous character, the cow-pie chomping cowboy from Cactusville, Desperate Dan. Drawn every week from 1937 to 1969 by Dudley Watkins, it was not until 1984, with No. 2243, that Desperate Dan took the coveted cover spot with art supplied by Ken Harrison.

In that first issue it was Korky the Cat who was the cover star, drawn by James Crichton until his retirement in 1962 when Charles Grigg successfully took over the role. Twenty years later, following Grigg's own retirement, David Gudgeon became the Korky artist.

Korky was a popular character, and the first editor of *The Dandy*, Albert Barnes (who was in the role from 1937 to 1982), was adamant that Korky was the cover star for his tenure. Korky's eternal battle with mice living in the skirting boards provided hundreds of laughs over the years, and if he wasn't at odds with the rodents, he would be trying to outwit the local fishmonger, gamekeeper or policeman with mixed results.

Korky's humanoid nature appealed to youngsters, and both he and Biffo the Bear became long-standing successes because children could relate to the fact that they had two arms and two legs. By contrast, the ostrich Big Eggo had (perhaps unconvincingly) hands at the end of his wings, and the strip fell out of favour with readers in the late 1940s after ten years on the cover.

It was no coincidence that the cover stars of *Beano* and *The Dandy*, chosen for the first issues and beyond, were predominantly black and white. Cover stars Big Eggo, Biffo the Bear and Korky the Cat contrasted well against brightly coloured backgrounds, appealing to children and successfully standing out on the news counter.

The covers of the two comics were instantly recognisable, particularly the title logos *The Beano Comic* and *The Dandy Comic* which are now considered iconic. In 1950 the word 'comic' was dropped, so readers looked out for *The Beano* and *The Dandy* at their local newsagent. Aside from the odd colour tweak and the adornment of the letters with snow for the Christmas issues, the title logos changed just a handful of times over the years. Two examples of such changes were in 1960 and 1971 when the comics were undergoing modernisation with extra pages and new characters.

Readers of *The Dandy* will remember a familiar presence to the left of the iconic title logo running until 1959. The anonymous bellboy seemed to present the comic to its readership much like they would welcome guests arriving at a hotel. *The Art and History of The Dandy* surmised that "*The Dandy* was intended to be seen as a sort of hotel for kids, a house of fun, and that the bellhop was their welcome party and guide."

The inclusion of creative and catchy slogans, which appeared at the top of both covers from the early 1940s, largely stopped after 1960. These slogans often came with accompanying snippets of artwork and were reintroduced in the 1970s.

One of the comics' biggest changes came during World War II when war shortages reduced both *Beano* and *The Dandy* in page number and size and forced them to run fortnightly rather than weekly. Still, both comics survived the war years and helped boost morale with propaganda covers mocking Hitler.

A number of free gifts were given away with the two comics before the war. Shortages sadly stopped the practice in 1940, and, with time, the popularity and high sales figures of the two comics meant that promotional free gifts just weren't necessary. In 1960 and 1971 though, as part of the comics' modernisation mentioned previously, free gifts were issued once again.

# A Cracker of a Christmas Number

From the 1930s to the 1970s, the process of producing a front cover strip for *Beano* and *The Dandy* involved several carefully followed steps. Firstly, the script writer (a member of the editorial team) came up with an idea for a script that was sent to an artist (either freelance or working as DC Thomson & Co., Ltd. staff) to mock-up as a pencil sketch. The editor would then review this sketch, and, once the story was depicted in the way the editor envisaged, the artist would draw the strip in ink.

The next step in the process involved the creative team at DC Thomson & Co., Ltd. who would add speech balloons and colour to the strip (interestingly, the colour was added as a reference mark to show the engravers and printers what colours were to be used where, and so often there was only a scribble of colour in each area). Once the work was ready, it was etched onto a printing plate to be inked-up and printed.

In the 1980s, the process of producing a front cover strip developed and became more digitised. The black and white artwork was digitally copied and coloured, creating colour negatives of each colour from which the final comic was printed.

It's fair to say that *Beano* and *The Dandy* have, over the years, become British institutions, and the various transformations that both comics have undergone since their inception has influenced our choice of covers for this book. We have, therefore, endeavoured to provide a cross-section of covers representative of each of the five decades.

As well as the No. 1 and 50th birthday issues, we have included in our selection several truly great fireworks covers – whizzing, whooshing and fizzling with fun – which offer some really striking artwork. The 1966 *Beano* fireworks issue, No. 1268, has always been a firm favourite of ours, and you can find it with the other *Beano* covers, running in chronological order, in the first half of this book.

Celebrated events throughout the calendar year, for example New Year, Easter and Halloween, have been included and so, too, have landmark editions, such as No. 500, 1000 and 2000, which celebrate these epic milestones in style.

*Beano* No. 931 features the work of legendary comic artist Leo Baxendale who drew some of his characters – mainly Little Plum and The Three Bears – for *Beano*'s masthead, accompanied by an eye-catching or witty slogan, from January to October 1960. These are a true delight, and we felt compelled to include an example in this book.

*The Dandy* No. 602, headlined 'Your Coronation Holiday Paper', is a celebration of the Queen's Coronation of June 1953, and we've included this cover for its uniqueness. *The Dandy*'s 1964 homage to The Beatles in No. 1158 (which devotes its cover story to The Beatles' song, 'She Loves You' and features The Fabulous Beatle Mice singing, "She loves cheese! YEAH! YEAH! YEAH!") has also been included for this same reason.

Other unusual covers chosen for this book include *Beano* No. 2396 which features three characters who don't normally grace the cover: Minnie the Minx, Ballboy and Billy Whizz. (Incidentally, this cover was recreated on Scarborough beach with the help of local school children during the same week as publication.) You will also find here the only issue in the forty-seven years of Korky the Cat's cover reign where Korky isn't present – keep an eye out instead for Keyhole Kate on the cover of *The Dandy* No. 295.

# KORKY THE CAT

"KORKY CAT, KORKY CAT, WHERE HAVE YOU BEEN?"
"I'VE BEEN TO LONDON TO SEE THE QUEEN."
"KORKY CAT, KORKY CAT, WHAT DID YOU THERE?"
"I CHEERED HER AND CHEERED HER FROM UP IN THE AIR."

Despite the inclusion of an array of striking single-panel covers, we have also chosen several that might, at first glance, be considered less impactful on the eye. These represent the more familiar style of cover that loyal readers have become so fond of when they buy their weekly comic, and it felt fitting to include a selection here.

Many examples of the differences between *Beano* and *The Dandy* can be found within this book. Though the pair were, in effect, companion papers, they have a different ethos and story construction. *The Art and History of The Dandy* comments that *The Dandy* makes greater use of comic violence to give someone a surprise or make them jump, so look out for boxing gloves on springs, escapades with fireworks, an exploding Christmas turkey, and even mice firing a cork from a cannon into Korky's mouth at point blank range.

Finally, as a special extra, we are delighted to showcase four original pieces of comic artwork shown opposite their respective front covers. (The original artwork for *Beano* No. 911 and *Beano* No. 1640 are both great examples of how front cover strips were produced from the 1930s to the 1970s, mentioned previously.) Our sincere thanks to Duncan Laird of the Archive Department at DC Thomson & Co., Ltd. for spending time diligently searching the stores and locating these pieces. To the best of our knowledge they have not been reprinted or seen by anyone other than DC Thomson & Co., Ltd. staff.

We would like to extend our thanks here to a small number of private collectors, named at the front of the book, who have very kindly searched their collections to provide us with cover scans of elusive comics.

This unique collection represents some of the most alluring, iconic and nostalgia-inducing covers from a classic fifty-year period in the history of *Beano* and *The Dandy,* and we hope you enjoy reading it as much as we've enjoyed creating it.

Best wishes,
Phil Shrimpton
September 2019
**www.phil-comics.com**

The following pages contain eighty *Beano* covers, chosen for this collection, in chronological order. In addition, the original artwork for No. 861, 911 and 1640 is shown opposite its final printed cover.

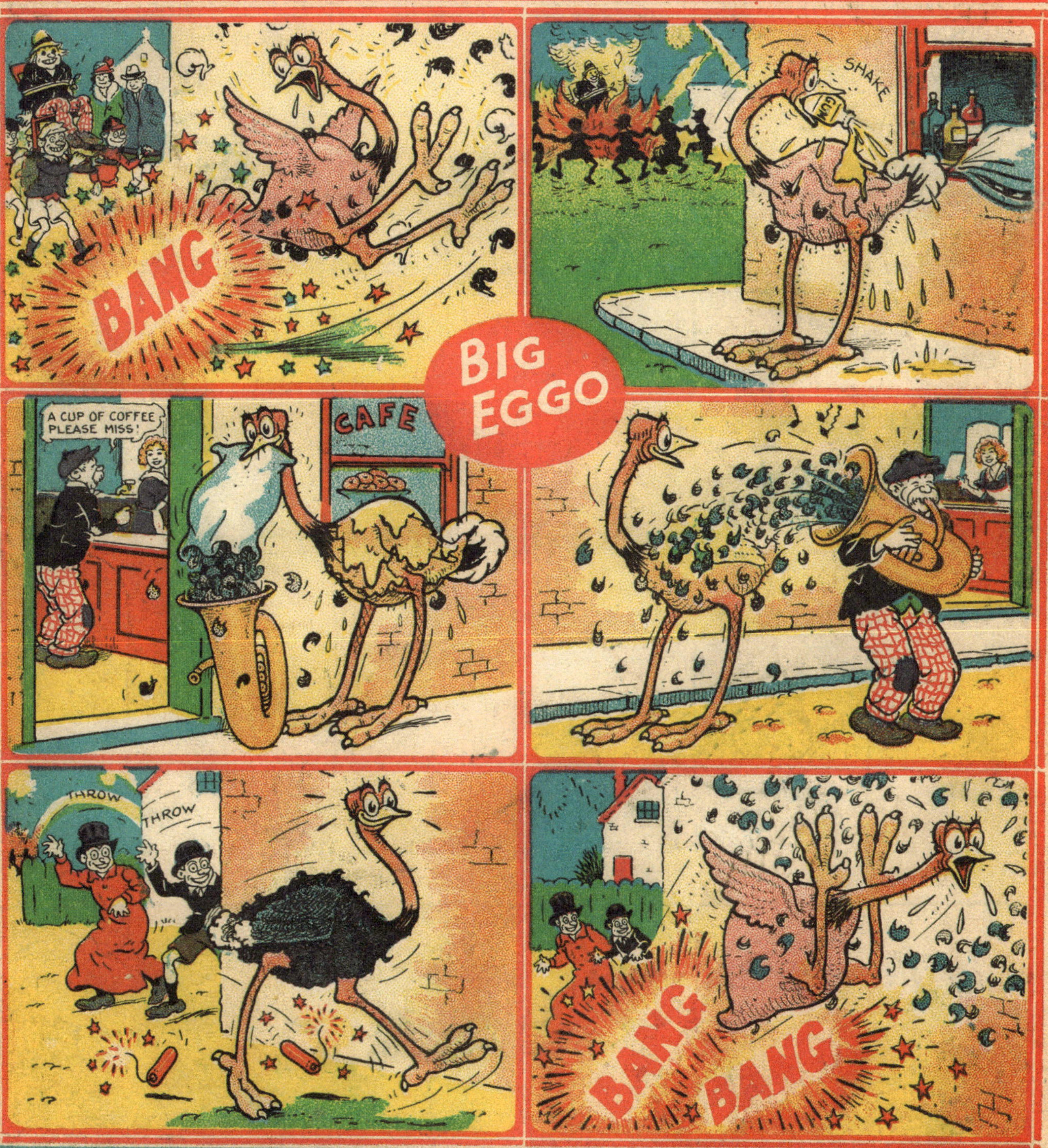

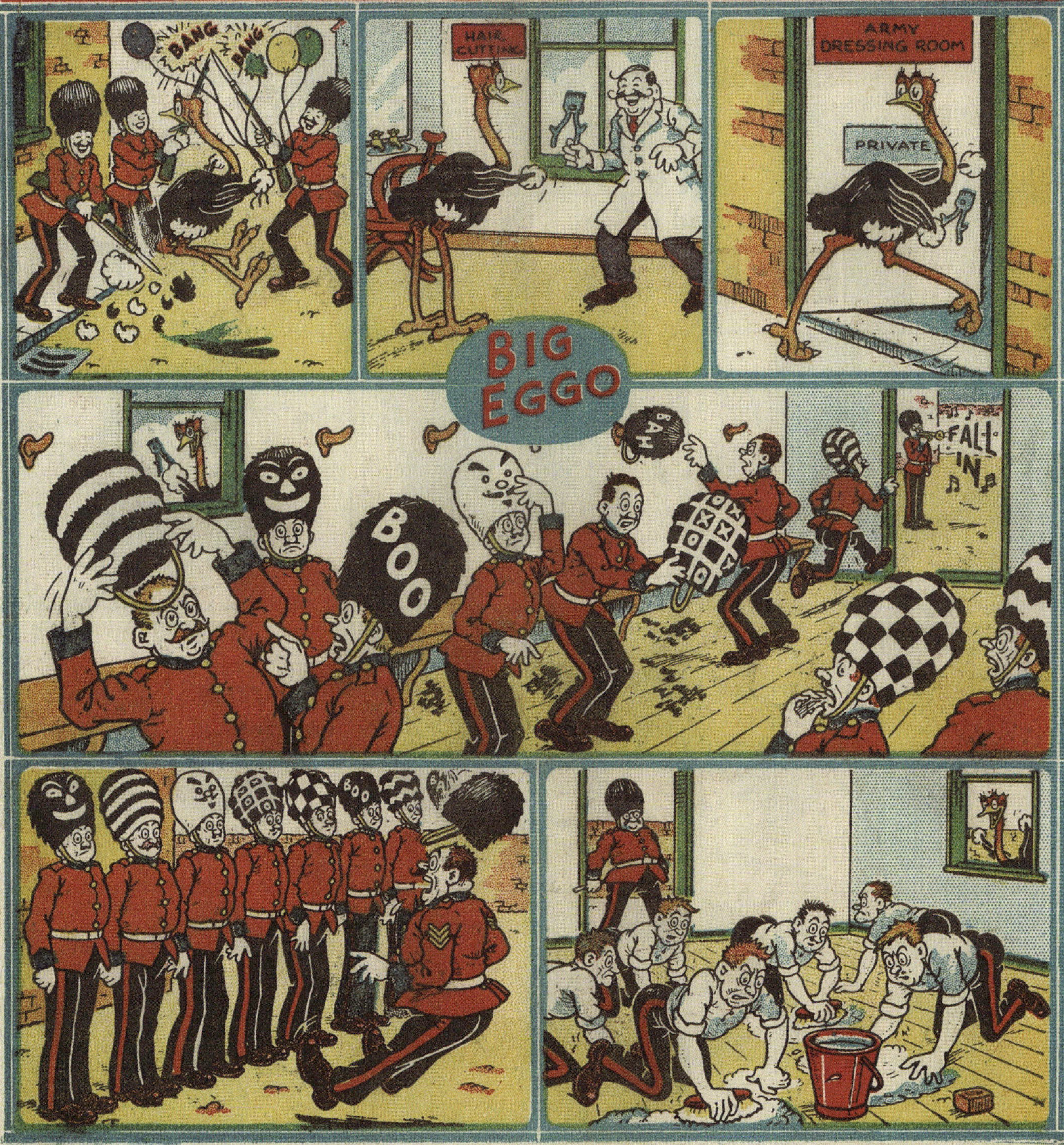

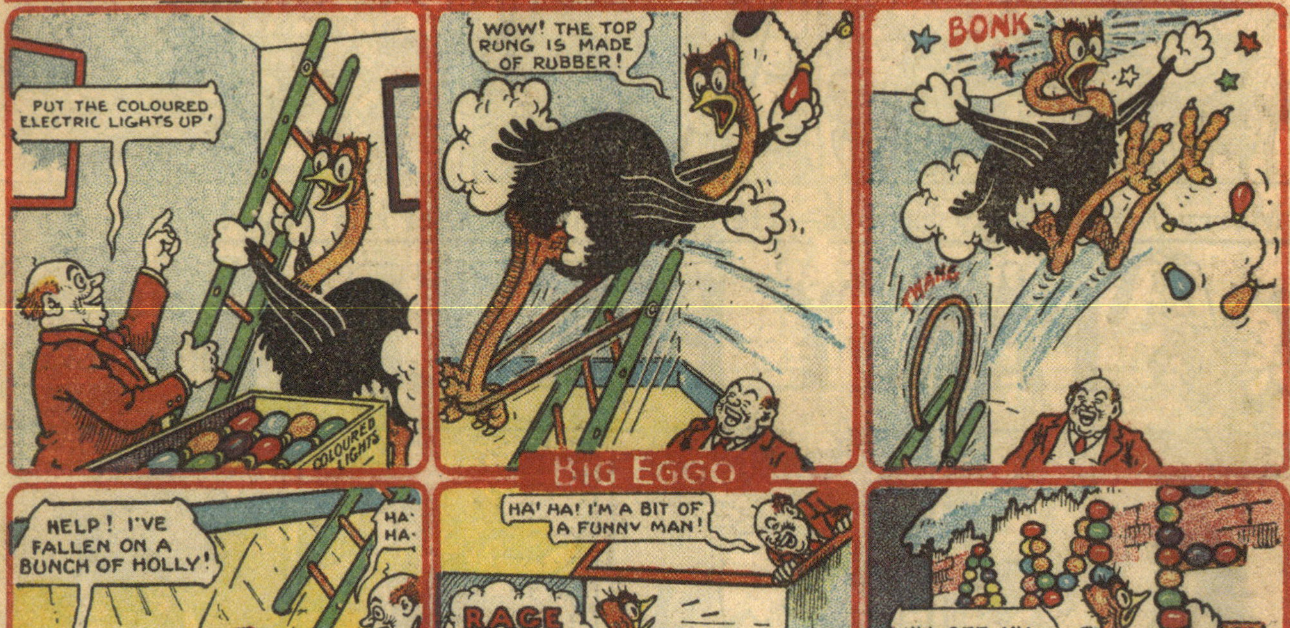

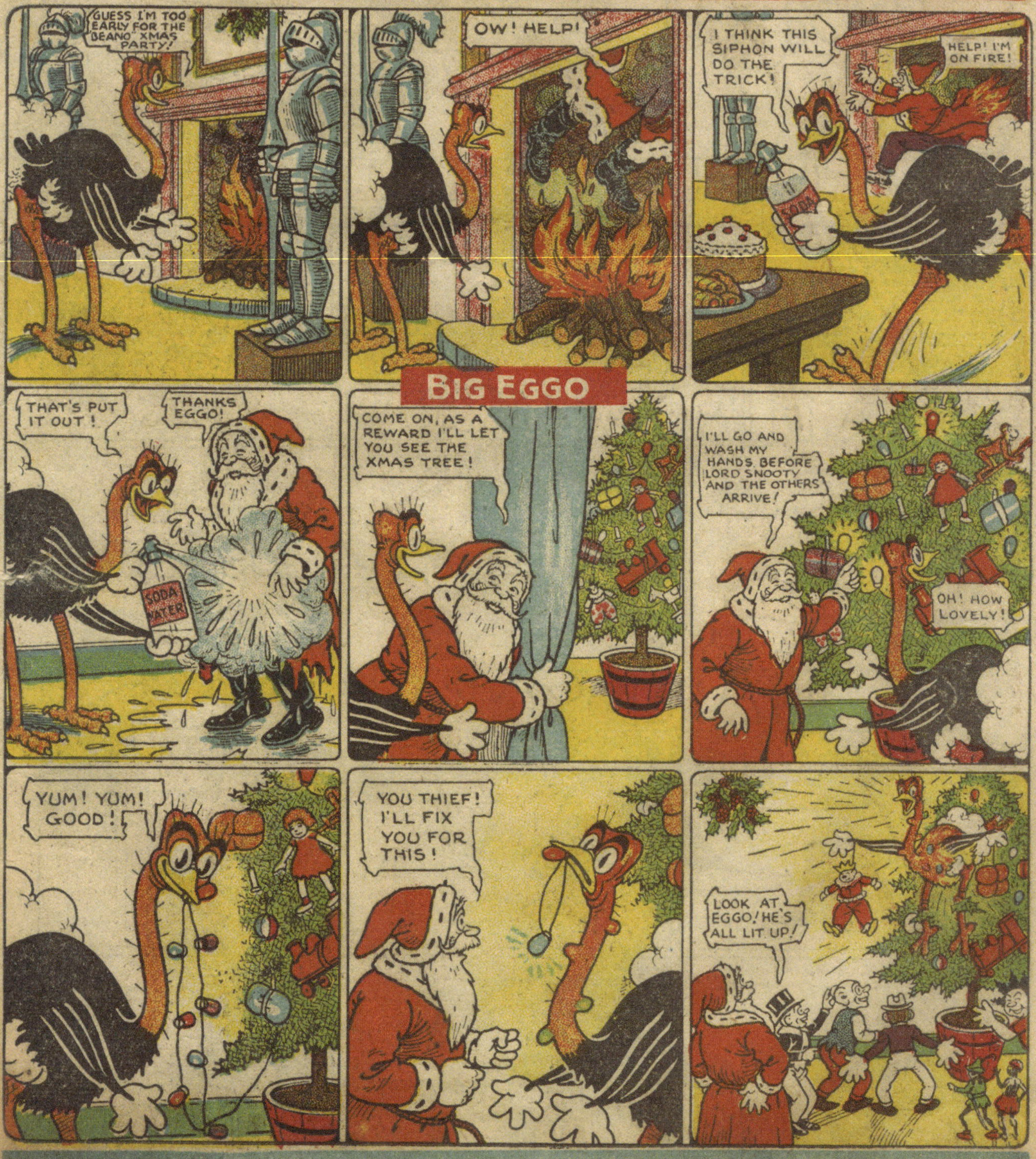

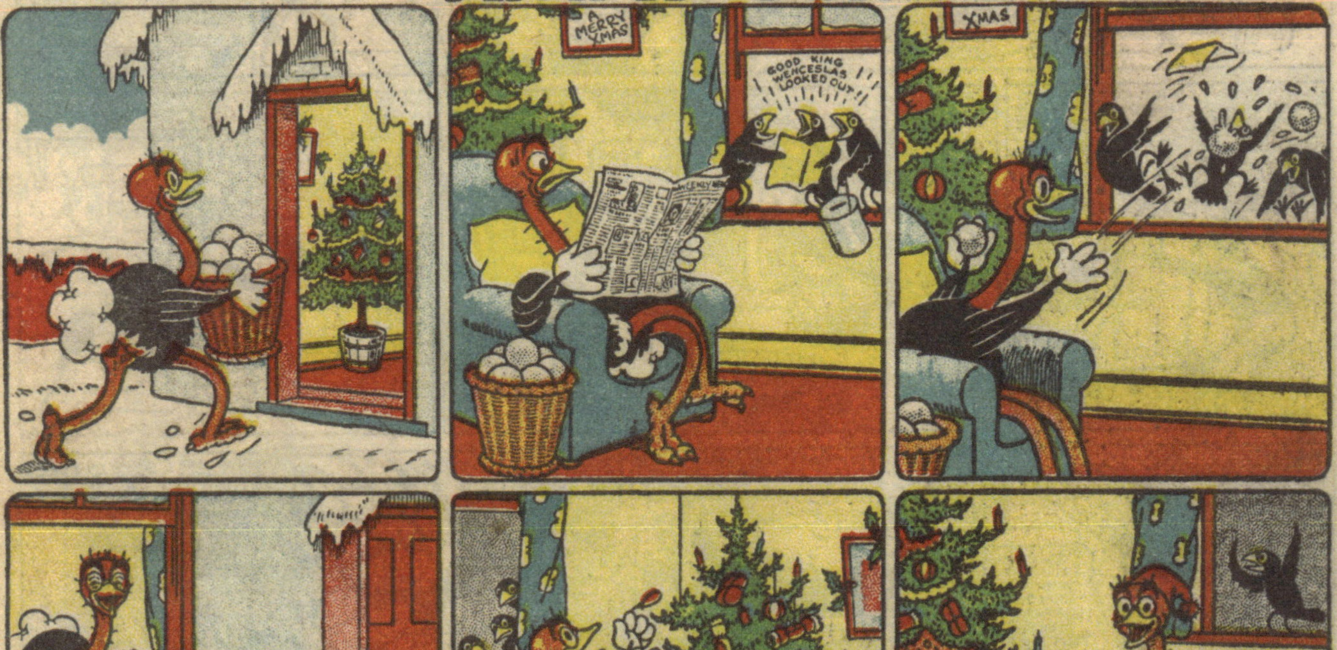

 —HIP HURRAH! HIP HOORAY! — **BIFFO BEAR is here to-day!**

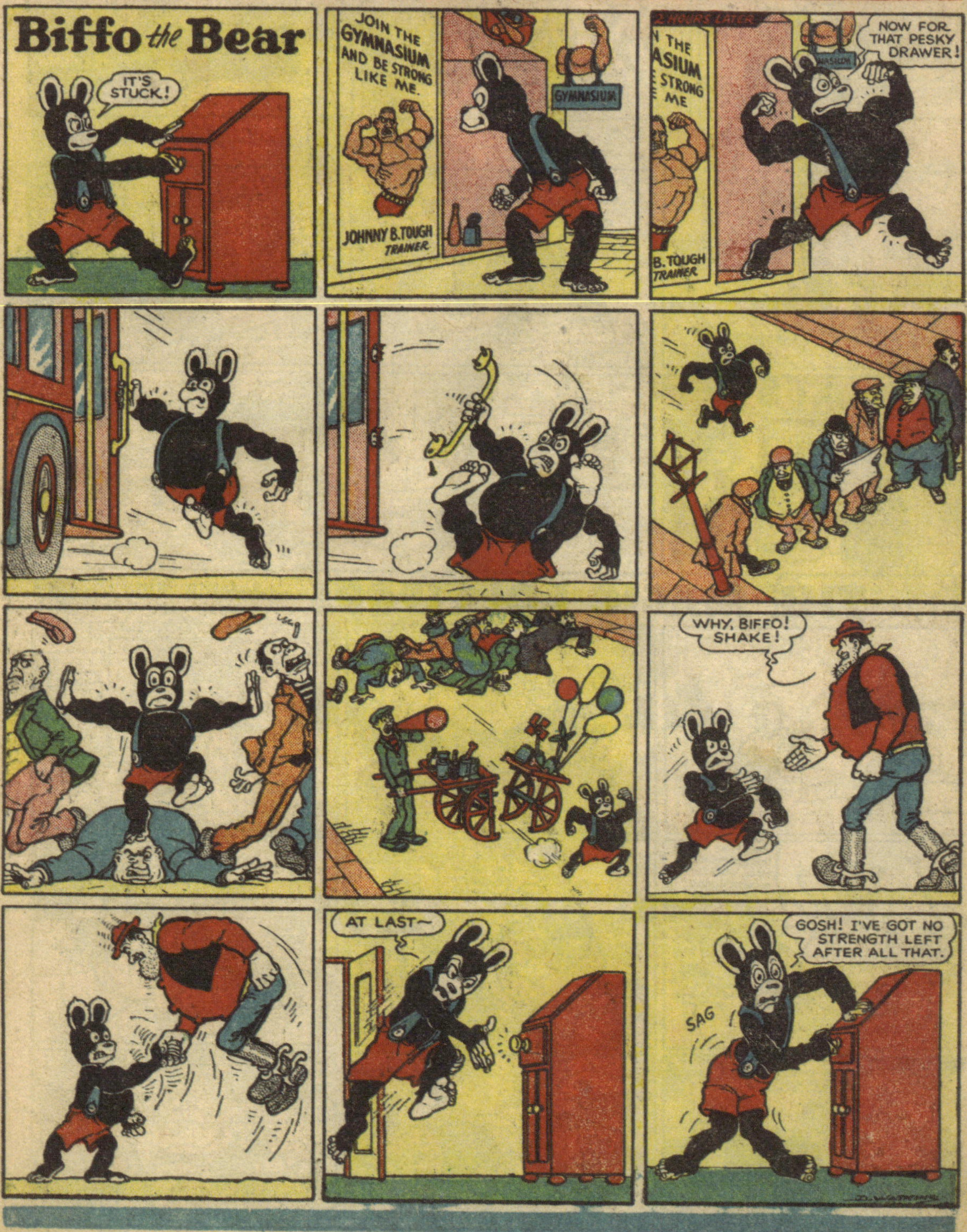

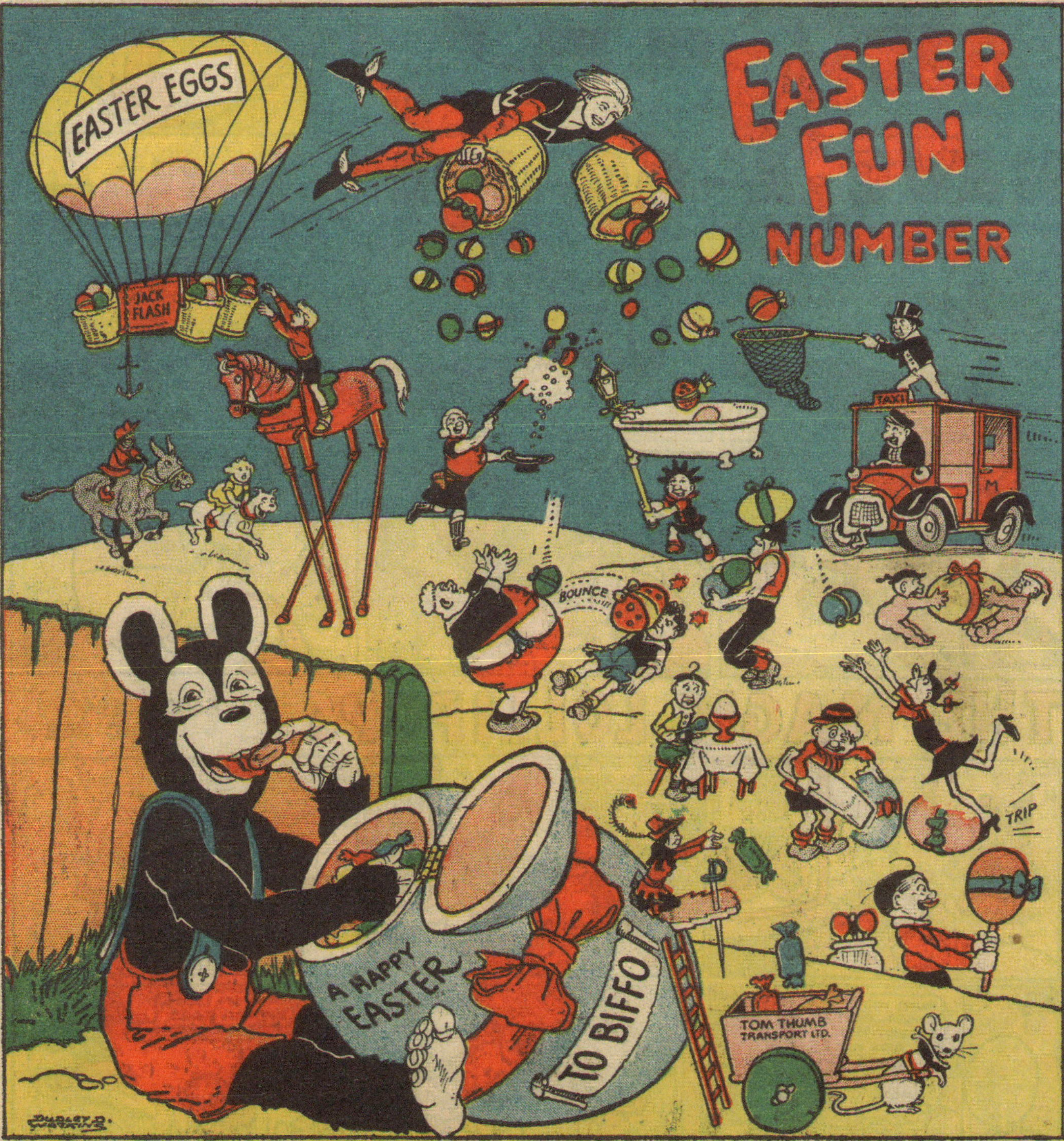

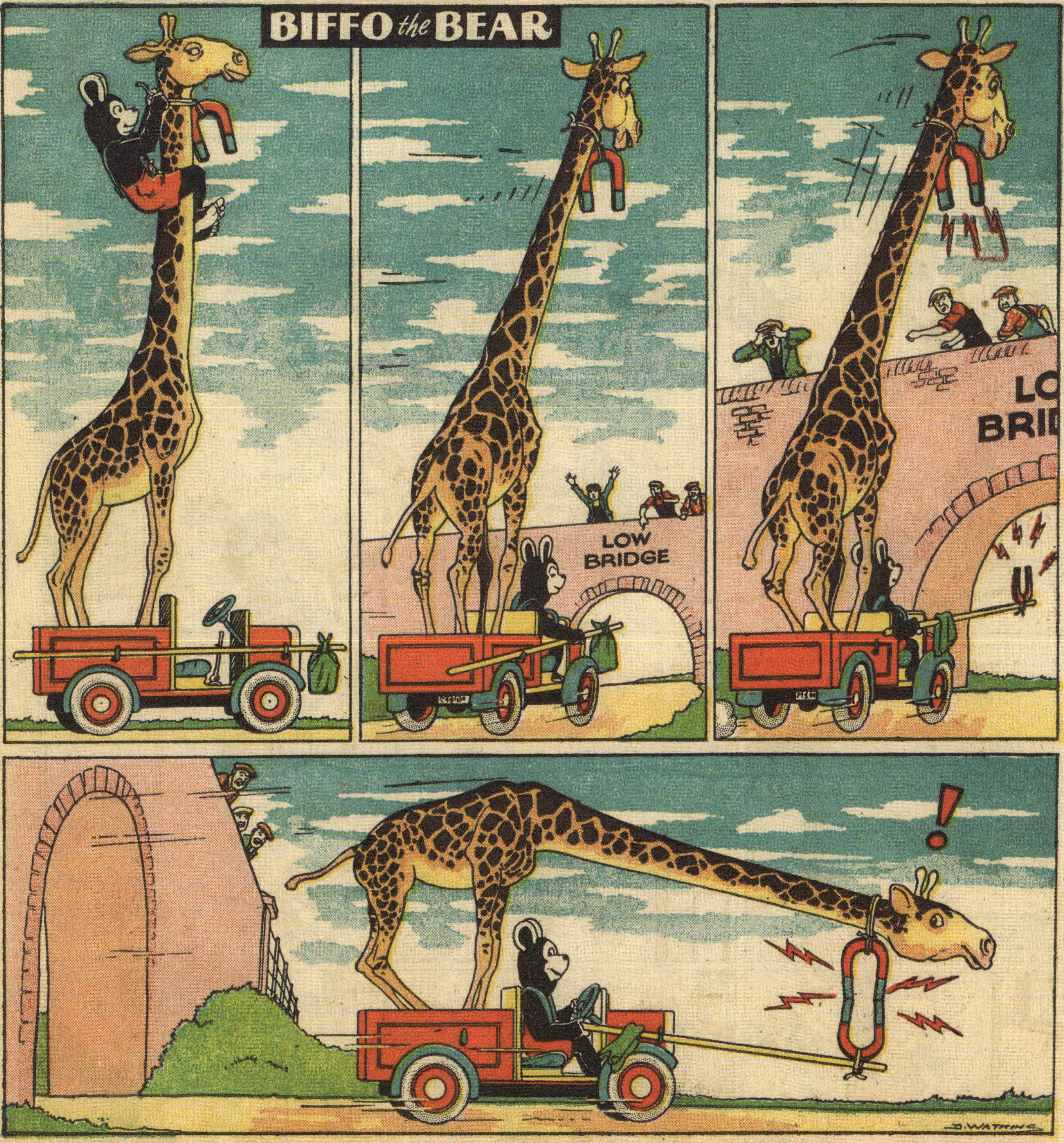

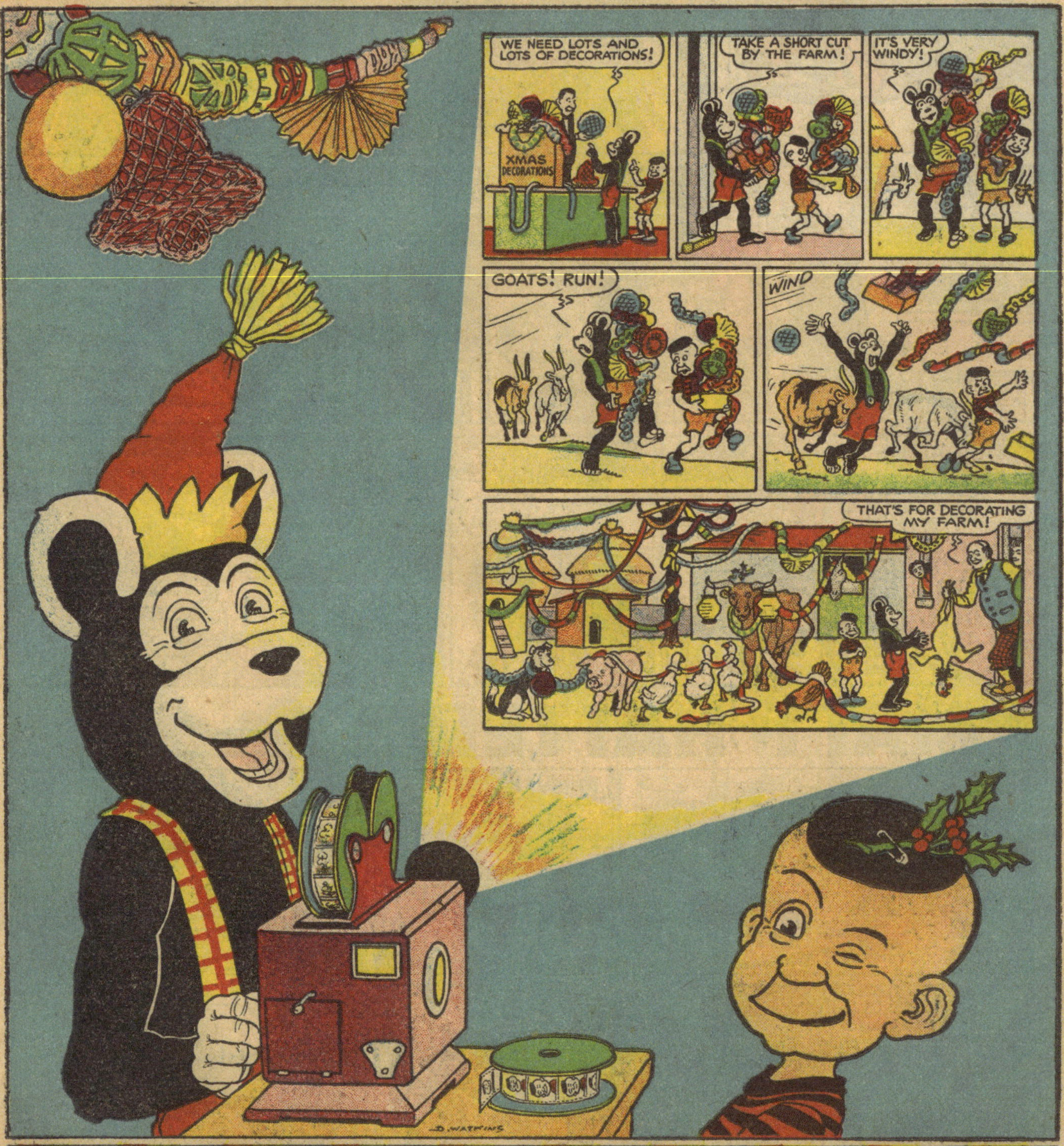

Spend a LAUGH-HOUR with "The BEANO" funsters


# THE BEANO

No. 861. Jan. 17th, 1959. 2d

EVERY THURSDAY

Be a BRIGHT SPARK and follow "The BEANO" The BEANO

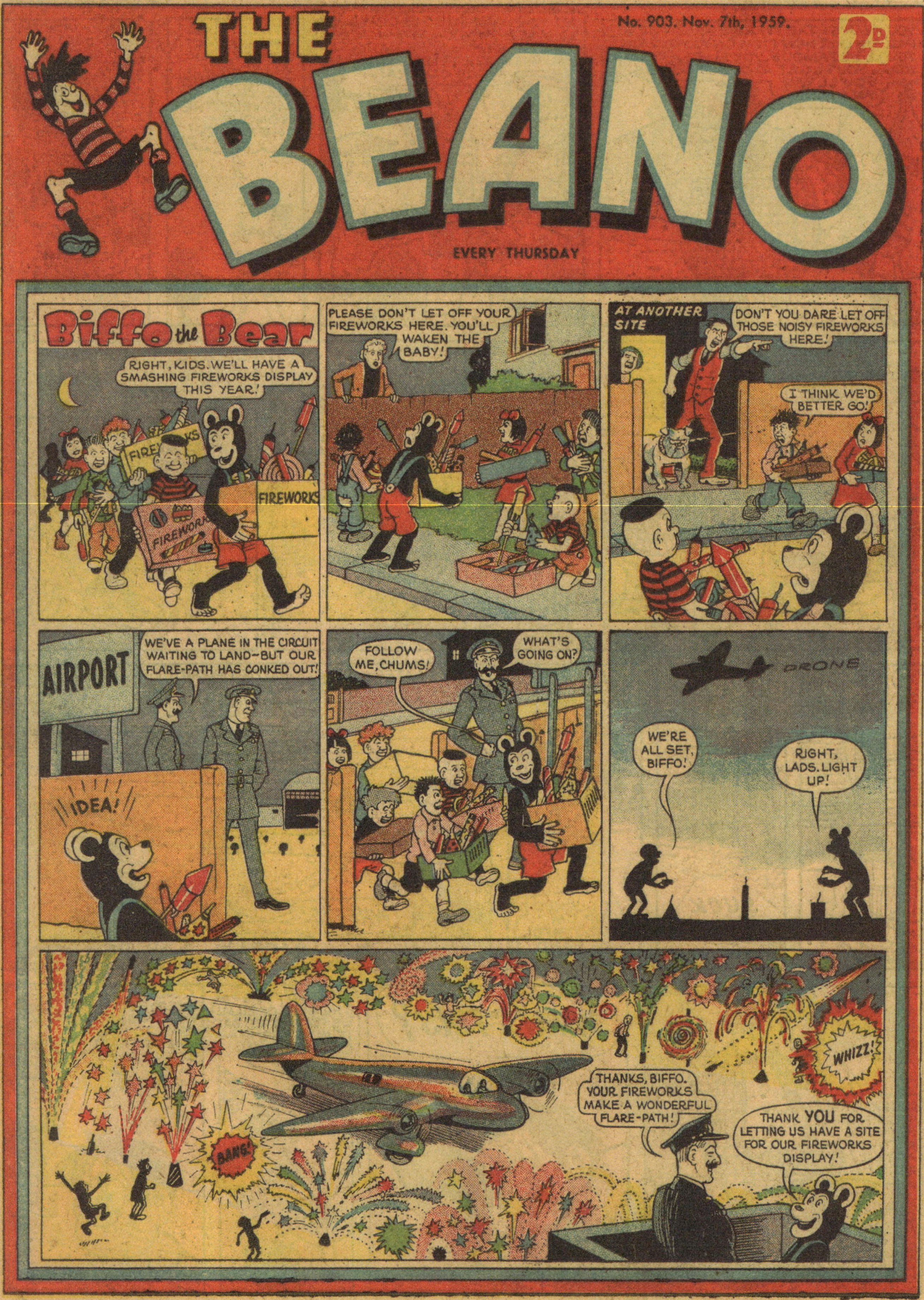

The BEANO, January 2, 1960

## Meet Sir Dennis Ye Menace INSIDE!

# THE BEANO

No. 911—Jan. 2nd, 1960. 2p

EVERY THURSDAY

### BIFFO the BEAR

I MUST HAVE A SHOT AT THE SKI-JUMP!

HERE GOES!

AGGH!

HELP

WE RATHER GUESSED YOU NEEDED HELP, BIFFO!

# KEEP AN EYE ON "THE BEANO" EVERY THURSDAY

THE BEANO

No. 931—May 21st, 1960. 2d

EVERY THURSDAY

A REAL BUMPER NUMBER!

No. 941—July 30th, 1960.

2d

# THE BEANO

EVERY THURSDAY

The BEANO, October 22, 1960.

# The Beano

**SUPER FREE GIFT INSIDE!**

EVERY THURSDAY — No. 953 — OCTOBER 22nd, 1960 — 3d

**BIFFO THE BEAR**

"THERE'S A..."

"THERE'S A SMASHING..."

"THERE'S A SMASHING FREE GIFT..."

"THERE'S A SMASHING FREE GIFT FOR YOU INSIDE"

BRRR—

SO HAVE FUN WITH THE **FLYING SNORTER!**

# The Beano

**The BEANO, December 10, 1960.**

*THE PAPER WITH JONAH!*

EVERY THURSDAY — No. 960—DECEMBER 10th, 1960 — 3¢

## BIFFO the Bear

"GOOD MORNING, ALL!"

"AARGH!"

"HELP! I'M GOING BACKWARDS!"

"KEEP PUSHING, FELLAHS!"

"NOW, ALL TOGETHER— HUP!"

"CAN'T YOU LET US SQUIRRELS SLEEP THE WINTER OUT IN PEACE?"

"GOOD NIGHT, ALL!"

The BEANO, December 24, 1960.

# The Beano

**HAVE A CRACKING GOOD CHRISTMAS HERE!**

EVERY THURSDAY — No. 962—DECEMBER 24th, 1960 — 3D

**BIFFO the BEAR**

"Look at that huge Christmas tree! It belongs to Mr Grump upstairs!"

"Oh, please, Mr Grump, would you give us just a tiny piece for our Christmas tree?"

"Nothing doing! I want it all for myself!"

**GLOOM!**

UPSTAIRS

"Huh! What a cheek! Cut a piece off this beautiful tree indeed!"

THUD!

"Help! It's going through the floor!"

CHRISTMAS DAY

"Serves you right, Meanie, for being so greedy!"

SNAP

WHOOPEE! "BEANO" NUMBER 1,000!

# The Beano

EVERY THURSDAY No. 1000—SEPTEMBER 16th, 1961 3D

THE "BEANO" CELEBRATION CAKE—CHOCK-FULL OF FUN!

# The Beano

**THE BEST BUY — BY FAR!**

EVERY THURSDAY — No. 1025—MARCH 10th, 1962 — 3D

## BIFFO THE BILLPOSTER

**Panel 1:** (Biffo carrying paste bucket, brush and bag marked "BEANO BILL POSTING Co. Ltd.")

**Panel 2:** HMMPH! WHAT AM I SUPPOSED TO DO WITH THESE?

**Panel 3:** I BEWA — I WONDER IF THIS IS CORRECT?

**Panel 4:** I BEWARE THE OAT BUN OVEN — THAT DOESN'T MAKE SENSE!

**Panel 5:** HE TRIES AGAIN. BUT NO BEAR IN THE WEAVE — THAT'S BARMY! AND ANYWAY I'VE GOT AN "O" LEFT OVER!

**Panel 6:** WHISPER-WHISPER! OH! I SEE!

**Panel 7:** NE... V

**Panel 8:** THAT'S IT, BIFFO! NEVER BE WITHOUT A BEANO — THANKS, PAL. IT MAKES GOOD SENSE NOW!

# The Easter Beano

**3D**

EVERY THURSDAY — No. 1031 — APRIL 21st, 1962

## BIFFO THE BEAR

**Panel 1:** THIS EASTER EGG FROM UNCLE JOE IS SO BIG THAT HE HAD TO SEND IT TO ME BY RAIL!

**Panel 2:** BAH! I'VE TRIPPED OVER A CAT!

**Panel 3:** THERE GOES MY PRECIOUS EGG — AND MAYBE IT'S FULL OF CHOCOLATES!

**Panel 4:** I'M CATCHING UP WITH IT!

**Panel 5:** NOW I JUST NIP IN FRONT AND STOP IT LIKE —

**Panel 6:** — THIS! UGH! IT'S GOING TOO FAST! WHUMP!

**Panel 7:** HELP! GASP! IT ROLLED RIGHT OVER ME! BOUNCE!

**Panel 8:** I MUST CATCH THAT EGG, OR THE CONTENTS WILL BE RUINED!

**Panel 9:** AH! GOT IT THIS TIME!

**Panel 10:** CLUNK!

**Panel 11:** OUCH! OOH! OW! SAVE ME! IT WON'T STOP! BIFF!

**Panel 12:** AT LAST! THANK GOODNESS I MANAGED TO JAM MY TOES IN THAT GRATING!

**Panel 13:** NOW TO SEE WHAT'S INSIDE.

**Panel 14:** OUCH!

**Panel 15:** BAH! ONLY A JACK-IN-THE-BOX! WAIT TILL I GET MY HANDS ON UNCLE JOE! KICK!

**Panel 16:** BUT WAIT! — THE HEAD'S MADE OF CHOCOLATE!

**Panel 17:** YUMMY! UNCLE JOE ISN'T SUCH A BAD CHAP AFTER ALL!

# The Christmas Beano

3D.

EVERY THURSDAY

No. 1066—DECEMBER 22nd, 1962

# The Beano

**3D**

EVERY THURSDAY
No. 1080—MARCH 30th, 1963

## BIFFO the BEAR

**MONDAY, 25TH MARCH, 1963.**
HIYA, BIFFO! I MET SNOOTY TODAY. HE SAID HE HADN'T SEEN YOU FOR A LONG TIME.
HM! THAT'S TRUE!

**TUESDAY, 26TH MARCH, 1963.**
I BUMPED INTO MINNIE TODAY. SHE SAID SHE HADN'T SEEN YOU FOR AGES.
YOU'RE RIGHT ABOUT THAT.

**WEDNESDAY, 27TH MARCH, 1963.**
I SAW THE BASH STREET KIDS TODAY. THEY WERE WONDERING WHERE YOU'VE BEEN HIDING YOURSELF LATELY.
I'VE GOTTA DO SOMETHING ABOUT THIS.

GIANT BIFFO BALLOON

HEH! HEH! I HAD IT SPECIALLY MADE. NOW **EVERYBODY** CAN SEE ME **ANYTIME!**

# The Beano

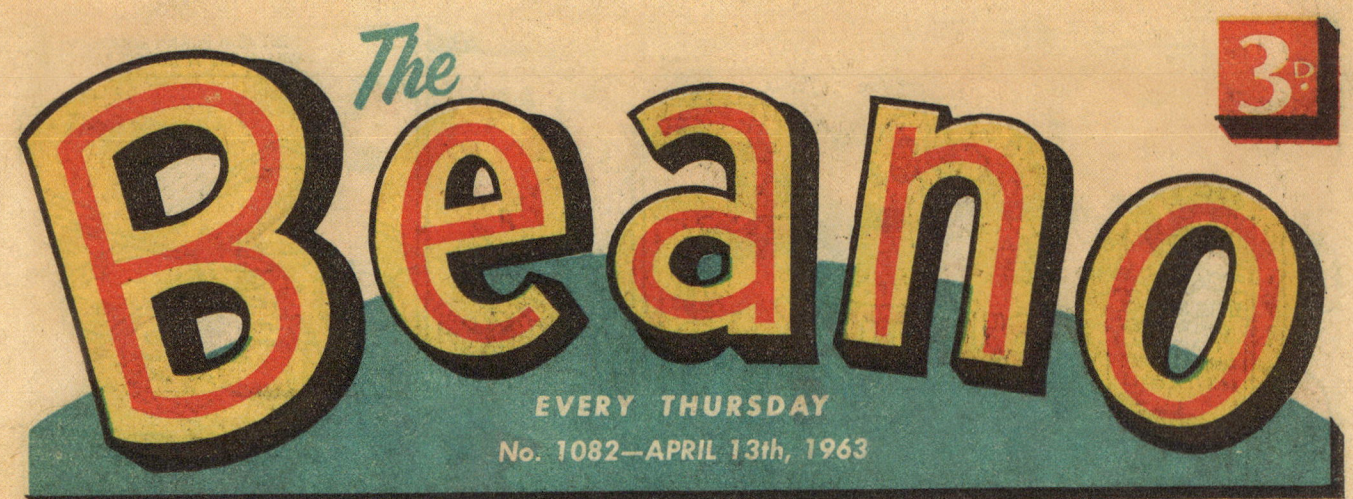

**Every Thursday**
No. 1082—APRIL 13th, 1963

**3D**

## BIFFO THE BEAR

- I'M HAVING AN EASTER PARTY TODAY!
- RAT-TAT!
- AH! WHO'S THIS?
- EASTER EGG FOR YOU, BUSTER!
- OOH! GOOD OLD BIFFO!
- From BIFFO to BUSTER
- WHERE'S BIFFO?
- I DON'T KNOW, BUT WE CAN'T START WITHOUT HIM. HE'S THE ONE WHO SENT THIS SUPER EGG!
- CRACK!
- WH-WHAT'S H-HAPPENING?
- HAPPY EASTER TO ONE AND ALL!

# The Beano

3D

EVERY THURSDAY

No. 1111—NOV. 2nd, 1963


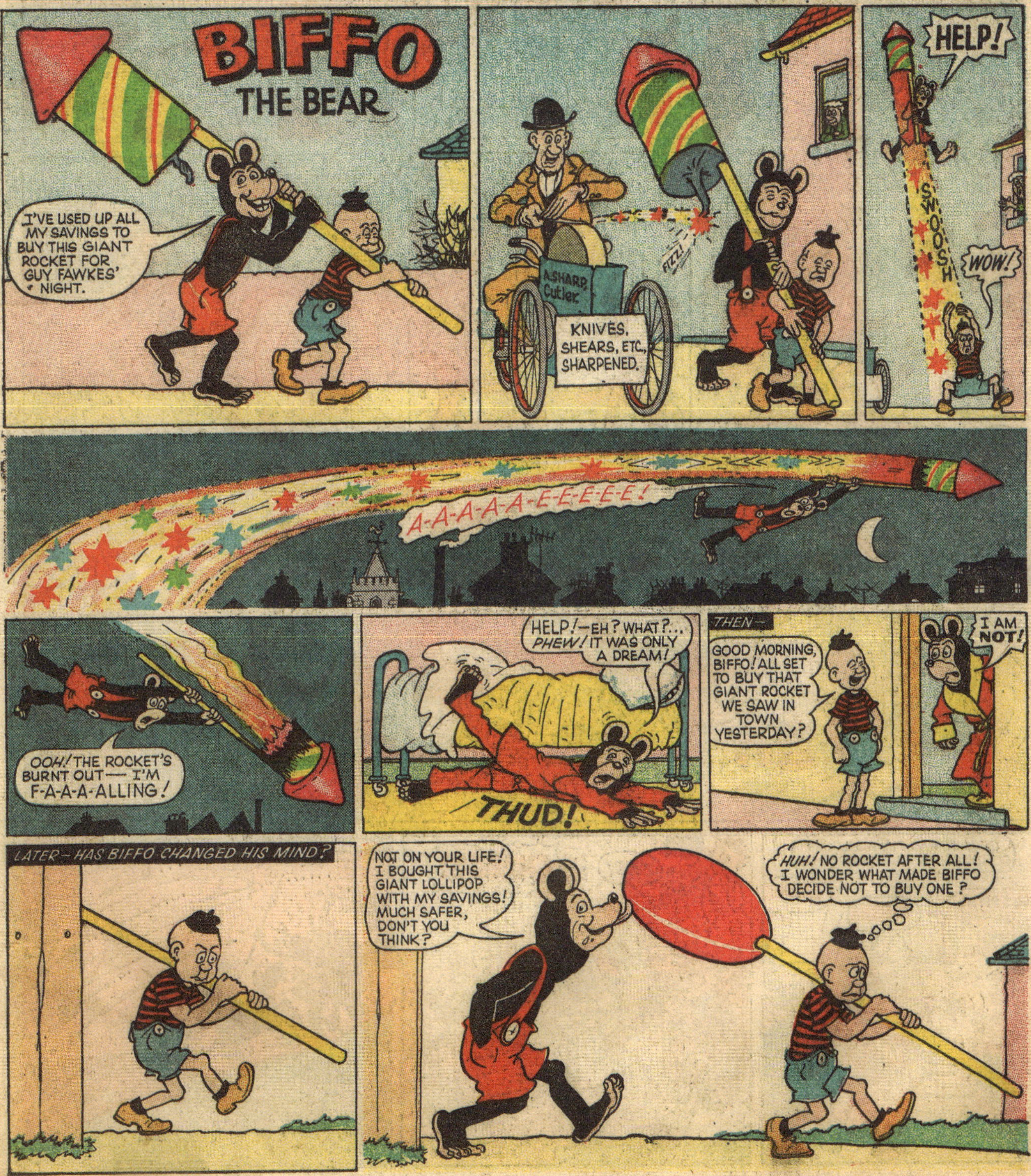

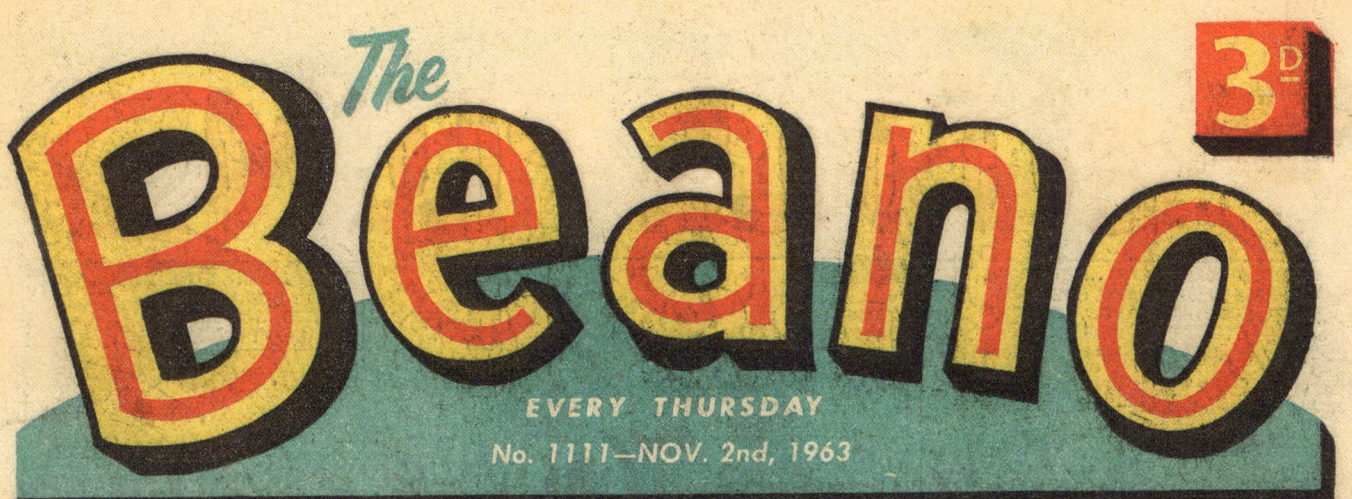

# The Beano

3d

EVERY THURSDAY

No. 1164—NOV. 7th, 1964

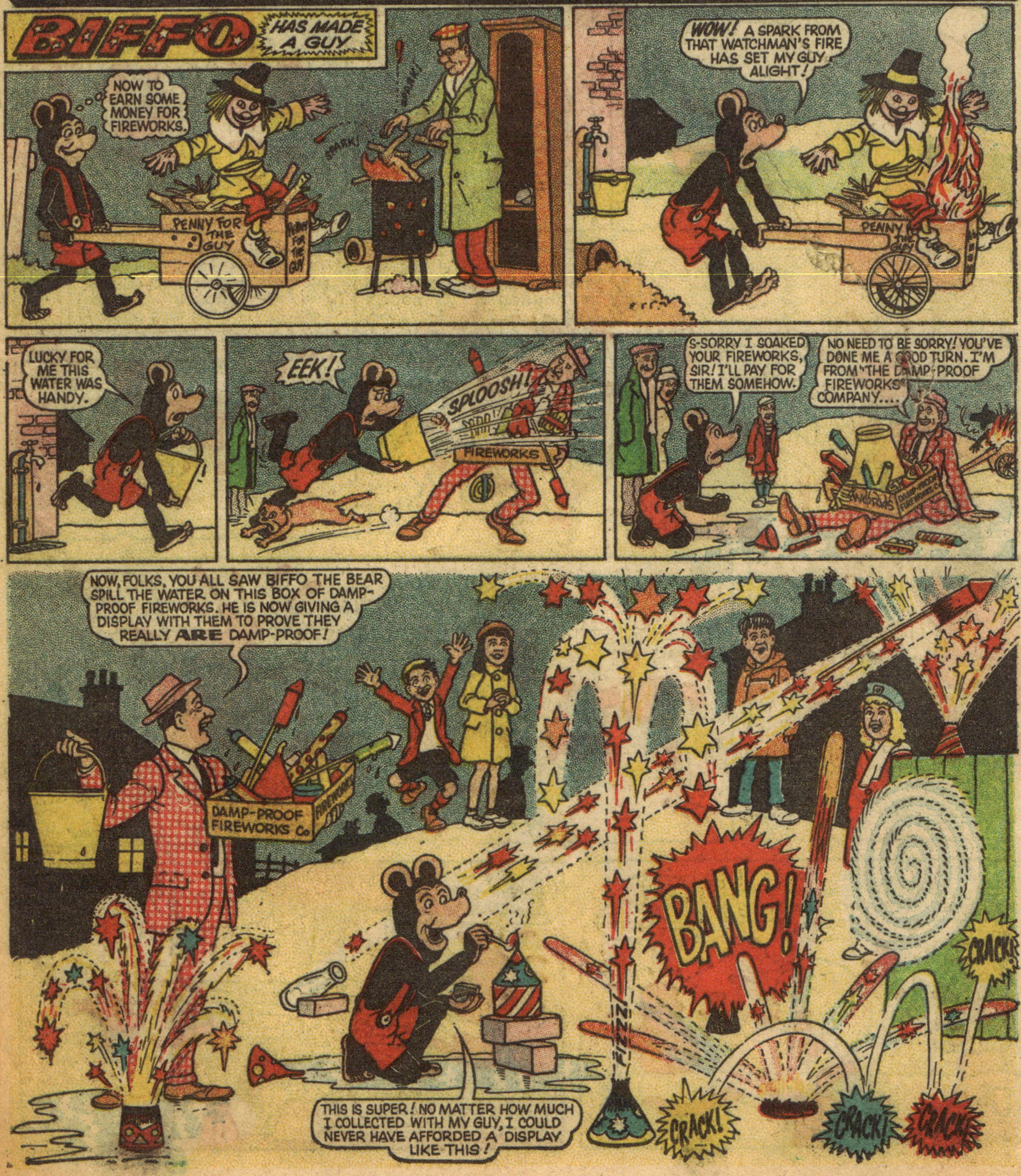

# The Beano

3D

EVERY THURSDAY

No. 1216—NOV. 6th, 1965.


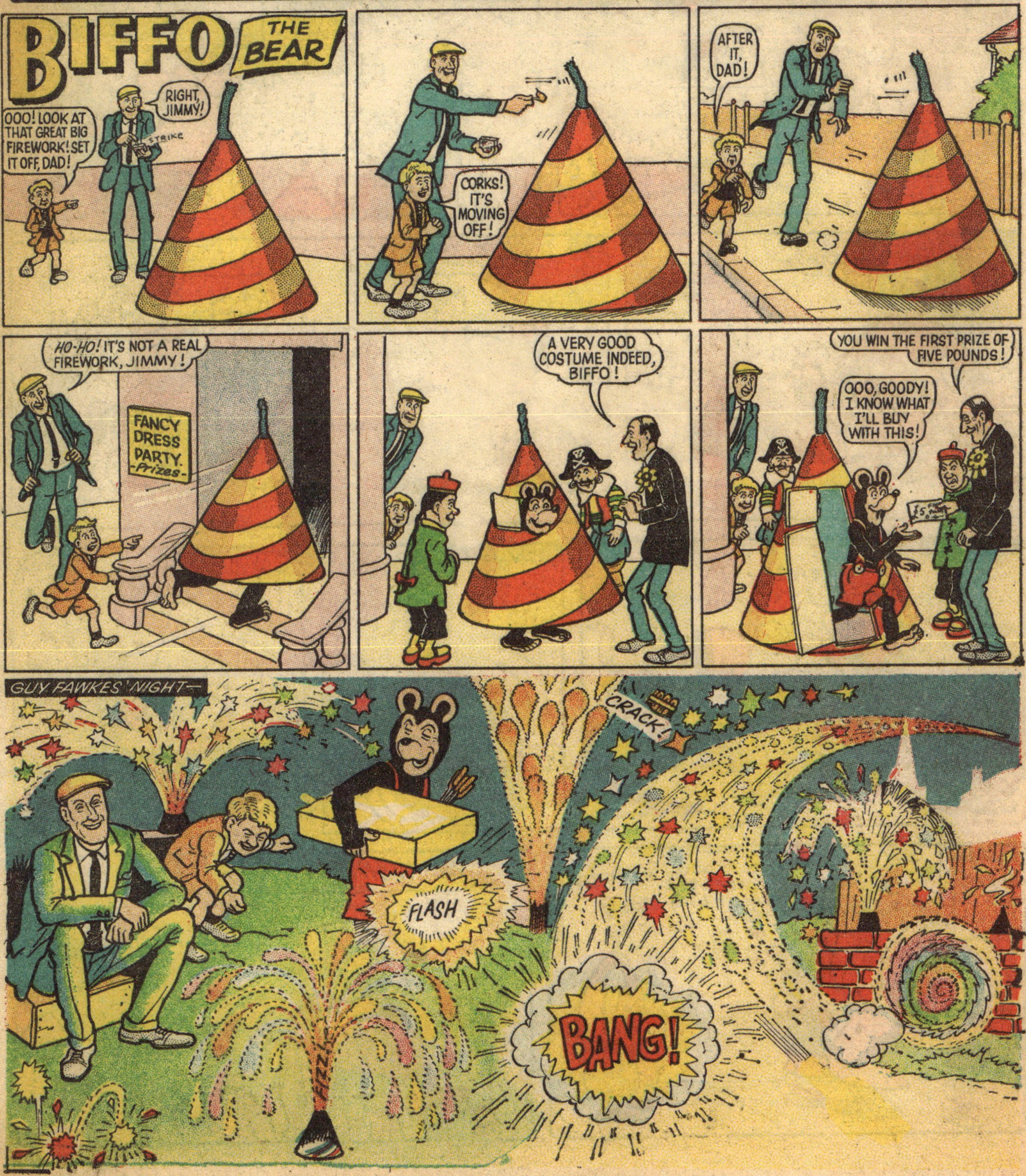

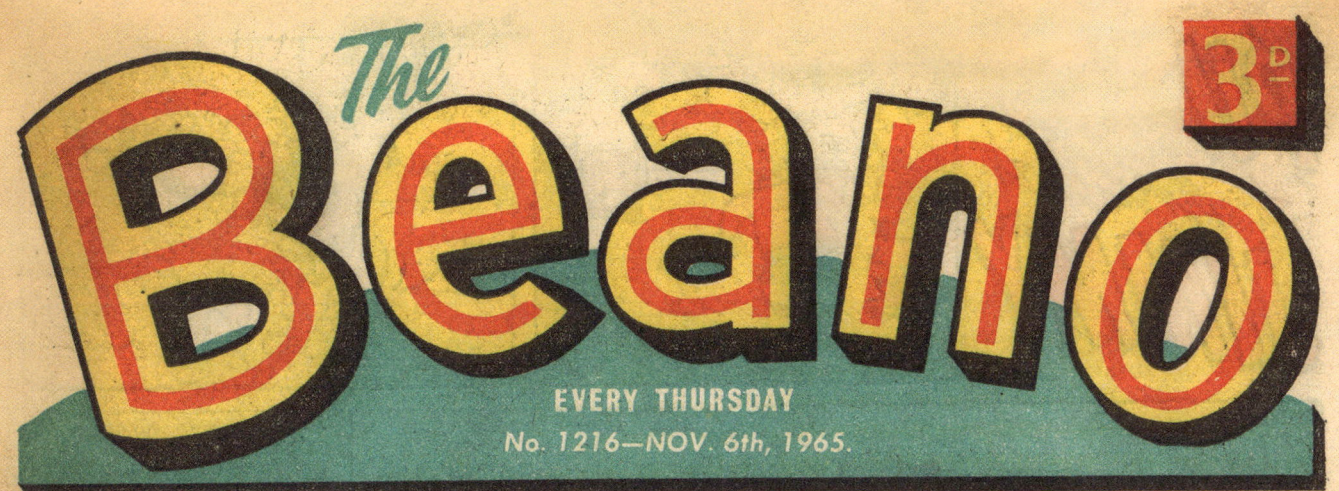

The

SUPER COMPETITION INSIDE

# Beano

EVERY THURSDAY No. 1238—APR. 9th, 1966. 3D

# The Beano

**3ᴅ**

EVERY THURSDAY
No. 1268—NOV. 5th, 1966.

## THE FUN GOES WITH A BANG INSIDE!

# THE CHRISTMAS Beano

EVERY THURSDAY — No. 1275—DEC. 24th, 1966 — 3D

**A MERRY CHRISTMAS TO ALL OUR READERS**

# The Beano

**3D**

Every Thursday
No. 1280—JAN. 28th, 1967.

## BIFFO THE BEAR

**POP!**

WHAT'S GOING ON?

EVERY THURSDAY
The Beano
No. 1292—APR. 22nd, 1967.
3D
The Bean
OH! THE "O"'S DROPPED OFF! IT JUST MISSED MY TOE.
CRUMP!
The Bean
STOP IT, SOMEONE!
PLOP!
LATER—
The Bean
JUST WHAT I NEED.
The Bean
HURRY UP, SONNY.
WHEE!
AT LAST—
THE BEANO PRINTING WORKS
The Beano
HERE WE ARE NOW.
The Beano
THANKS, BIFFO.
IT WAS A PLEASURE.

# The Beano

**3D**

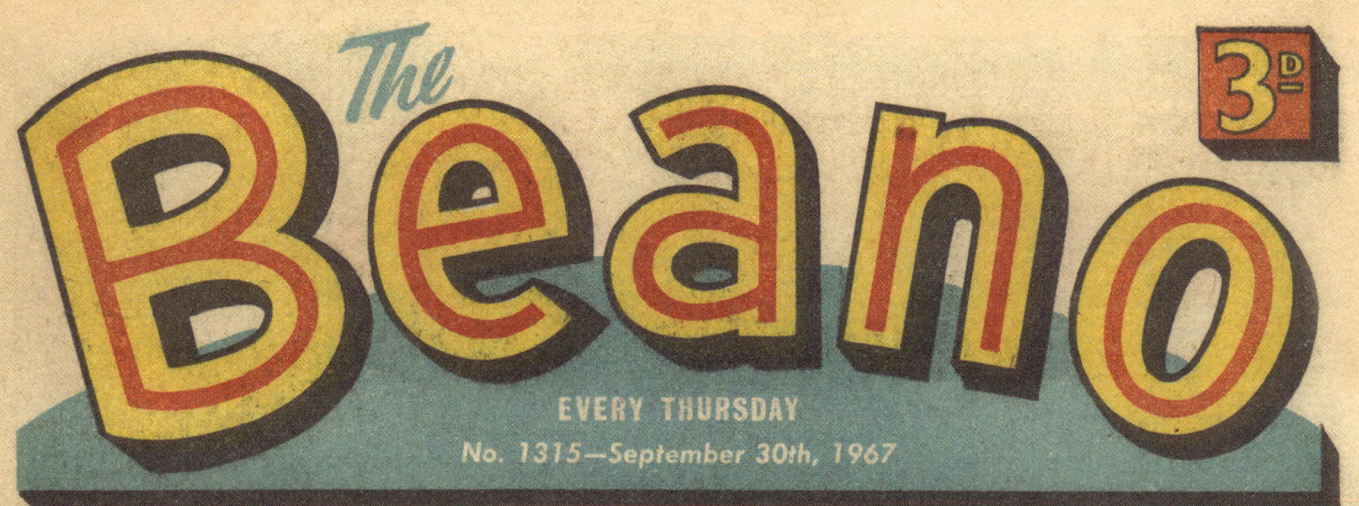

Every Thursday

No. 1315—September 30th, 1967

## BIFFO THE BEAR

"How do you like my new motor scooter, Buster?"

"Super, Biffo!"

"Now for a trial spin."

"Wow! Oo-er!"

"Look out!"

"You've done it!"

**CRASH!** RRIP!

"I've seen that picture before somewhere! Now where was it?"

"Ah, yes, that was it—the cover of this year's 'Beano Book'!"

"Hurry, readers! Scoot down to your newsagent and order your copy now!"

The Beano BOOK 1968

# The Beano

3D

EVERY THURSDAY

No. 1319—October 28th, 1967


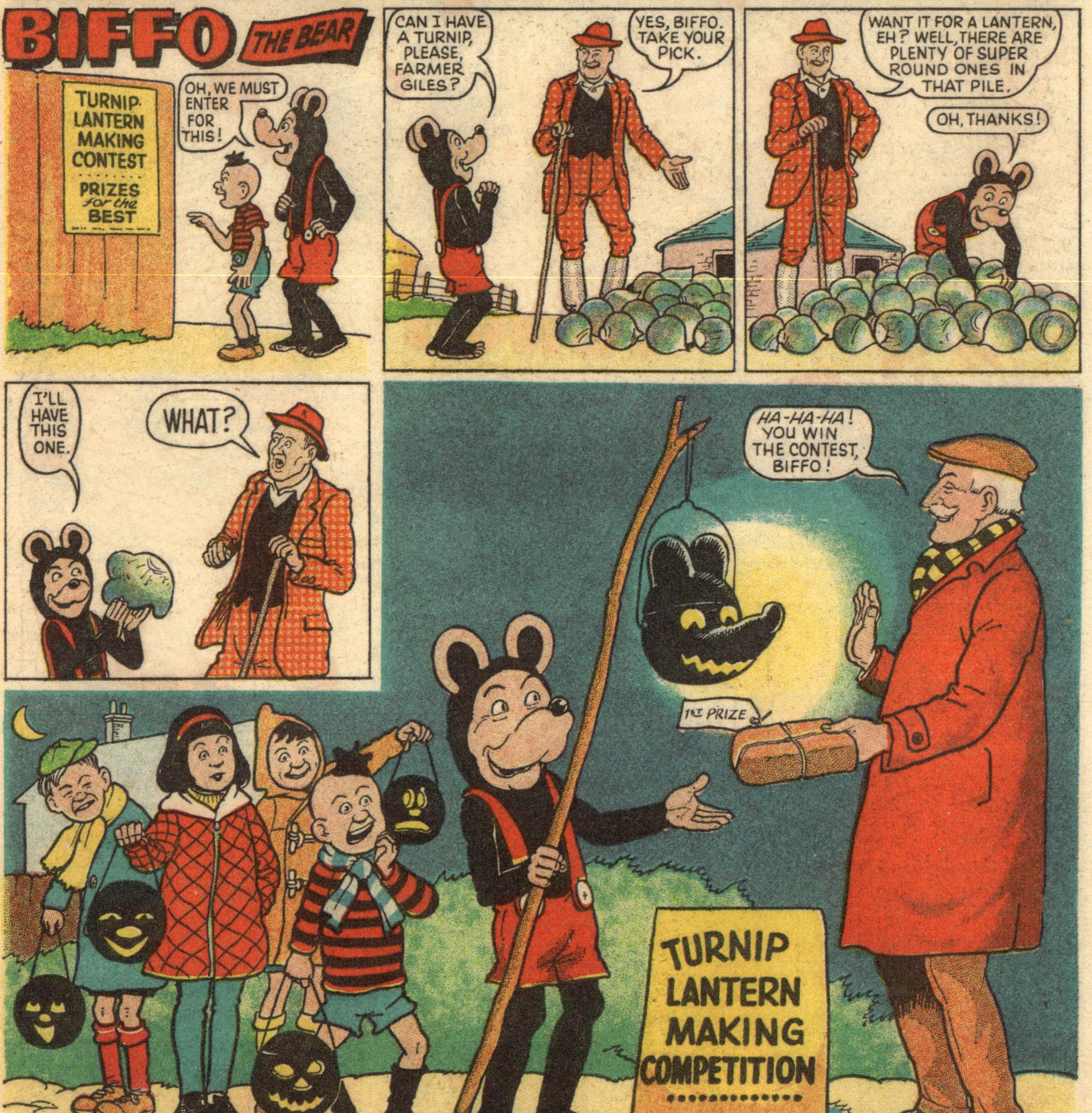

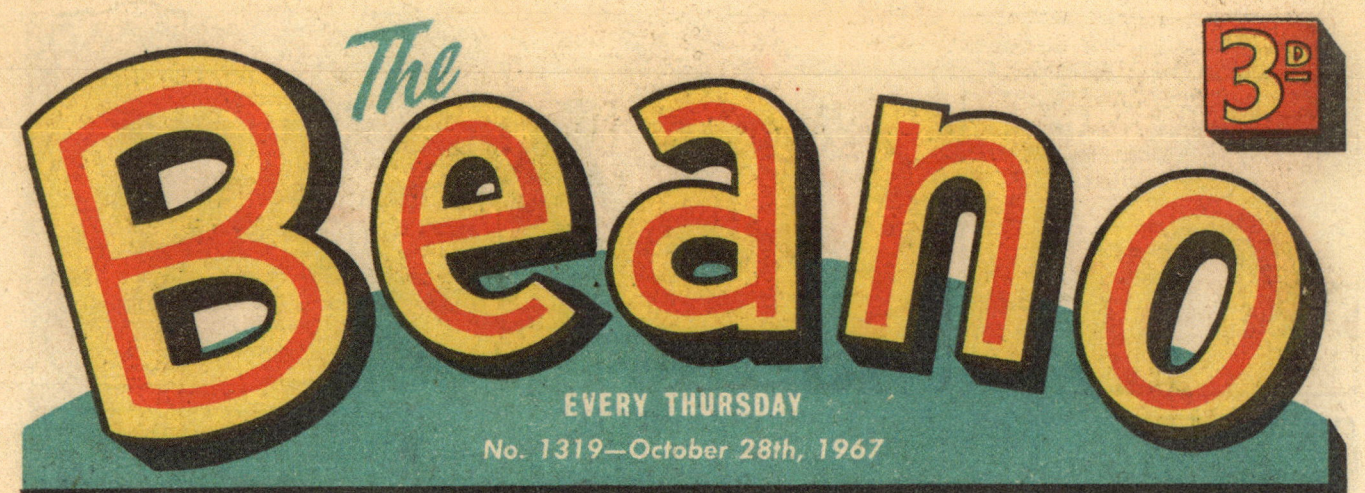

# The Beano

**4ᵈ**

EVERY THURSDAY
No. 1343—April 13th, 1968.

## BIFF THE BEAR

**Boy:** HI, BIFFO! YOU'RE LOOKING HOT!

**Biffo:** NO WONDER, I DON'T THINK I'VE GOT THIS MIXTURE RIGHT.

**Boy:** HM! AND YOU'RE LOOKING CROSS, TOO.

**Biffo:** YES, I AM HOT, AND I'M CROSS TOO!

**Boy:** WHAT ARE YOU MAKING?

**Biffo:** HOT CROSS BUNS OF COURSE!

# The Beano

**4D**

Every Thursday
No. 1406—June 28th, 1969.

## BIFFO THE BEAR

**1969 JUNE 27**

H'M! THAT'LL BE TO REMIND ME OF SOMETHING SPECIAL. I WONDER WHAT IT WAS?

IT MUST HAVE BEEN VERY SPECIAL OR I WOULDN'T HAVE MARKED IT ON THE CALENDAR!

WHAT COULD IT HAVE BEEN THAT WAS SO SPECIALLY SPECIAL?

HA-HA-HA! HEE-HEE-HEE!

WHAT'S ALL THAT MERRIMENT ABOUT?

SILLY ME! TAKE THAT—*OUCH!* HOW COULD I HAVE FORGOTTEN?

KICK

TODAY'S THE DAY "THE BEANO SUMMER SPECIAL" COMES OUT! DON'T FORGET TO PICK UP YOUR COPY, READERS!

**NEWSAGENT**

HAW! HAW! HAW!

THE BEANO SUMMER SPECIAL SOLD HERE

**The Beano SUMMER SPECIAL**

WHAT'S ALL THIS ABOUT? SEE BACK PAGE.

# The Beano

4d

Every Thursday
No. 1416—September 6th, 1969.

THIS IS A COPY OF THIS YEAR'S SUPER "BEANO BOOK." READ ON TO FIND OUT WHAT HAPPENED TO BIFFO AND HIS LOLLY.

THE BEANO Book 1970

GURGLE

HOI! SHOO!

TEE-HEE! THIS ICE-AXE COMES IN HANDY.

WATCH IT, BUSTER.

OOPS! NOW IT'S MELTING.

MY LOLLY WAS A BIG DISAPPOINTMENT, READERS, BUT YOU WON'T BE DISAPPOINTED IF YOU GET THE SUPER "BEANO BOOK".

FIRE-WOOD MERCHANT

# The Beano

4d
EVERY THURSDAY
No. 1440—February 21st, 1970.

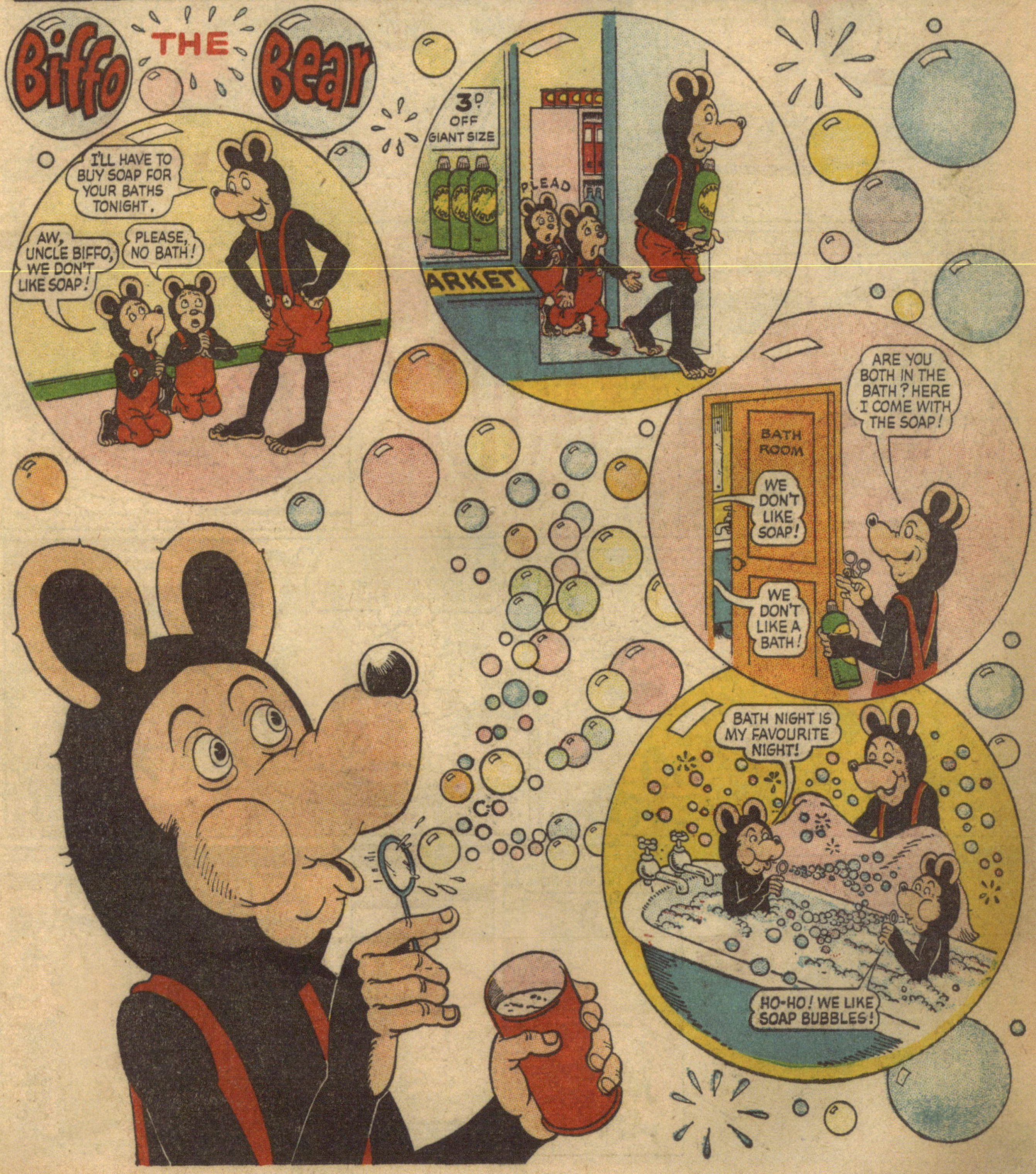

# The Beano

**EVERY THURSDAY**
No. 1445—March 28th, 1970.

**4D**

BIFFO the BEAR

HAPPY EASTER, READERS!

TWEET! TWEET!

THE CHRISTMAS
Beano
EVERY THURSDAY
No. 1484—Dec. 26th, 1970.
4D
WE WISH YOU A
MERRY CHRISTMAS
AND A
HAPPY NEW YEAR
CAROLS
CAROLS
CAROLS
CAROLS

# THE BEANO

**HAPPY EASTER, EVERYBODY!**

No. 1499—April 10th, 1971.  EVERY THURSDAY **2p**

## BIFFO the BEAR

BIFFO, THE EDITOR HAS SENT YOU AN EASTER EGG!

"BEANO" REMOVALS

OH, GOODY!

TO BIFFO

COO! WHAT A WHOPPER! I'LL HAVE TO GET ALL MY "BEANO" PALS TO HELP ME ROLL IT!

BUT— I CAN'T FIND ANY OF MY PALS—I'LL JUST HAVE TO ROLL IT ALONE! GRUNT!

WHOOPEE!

HOORAY! ALL MY PALS HAVE TURNED UP — NOW FOR A SUPER EASTER PICNIC!

# THE BEANO

The Comic With "LORD SNOOTY"!

No. 1520 SEPT. 4th, 1971. EVERY THURSDAY 2p

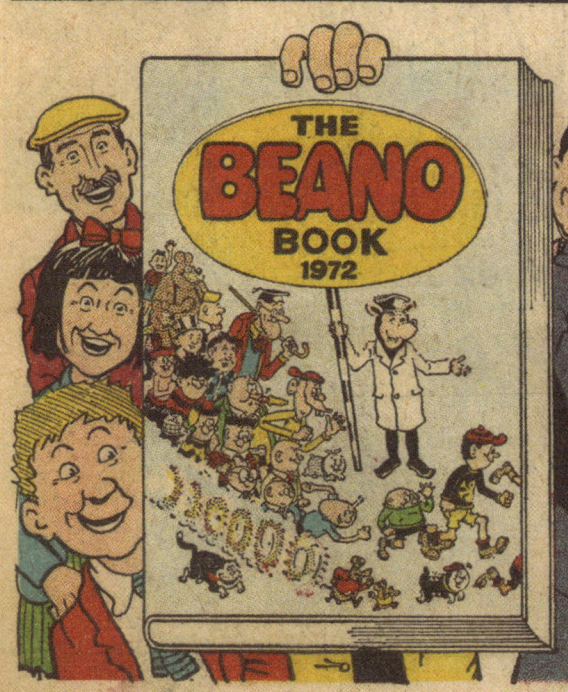

## BIFFO THE BEAR

GREAT BOOK SALE TODAY

INSIDE— "THIS RARE BOOK SOLD TO THIS GENTLEMAN FOR £30,000!"

AT ANOTHER STALL— "I'LL HAVE ONE OF EACH, PLEASE."

LATER— "THERE HE IS!" "HM! I'LL BET THEY ALL WANT TO SEE MY VALUABLE BOOK!"

BUT— "HM! BIFFO MUST HAVE BOUGHT SOME VALUABLE BOOKS!" "LET US SEE YOUR BOOKS, BIFFO!"

"YES, READERS! THESE BOOKS ARE WORTH THEIR WEIGHT IN LAUGHS!"

THE BEANO BOOK 1972

DENNIS the MENACE 1972

ON SALE NOW!

# THE BEANO

FREE Gift Inside—The FLYING FIZZER

No. 1522—SEPT. 18th, 1971. EVERY THURSDAY 2p

# The Christmas BEANO

No. 1536 DEC. 25th, 1971. EVERY THURSDAY 2p

A MERRY CHRISTMAS TO ALL OUR READERS

THE BEANO
The Comic With "MINNIE the MINX"!
No. 1550—APRIL 1st, 1972. EVERY THURSDAY 2p

THE *The Comic With "DENNIS the MENACE"!*

# BEANO

No. 1572 SEPT. 2nd, 1972. EVERY THURSDAY 2p

# THE CHRISTMAS BEANO

No. 1588—DEC. 23rd, 1972. EVERY THURSDAY 2p

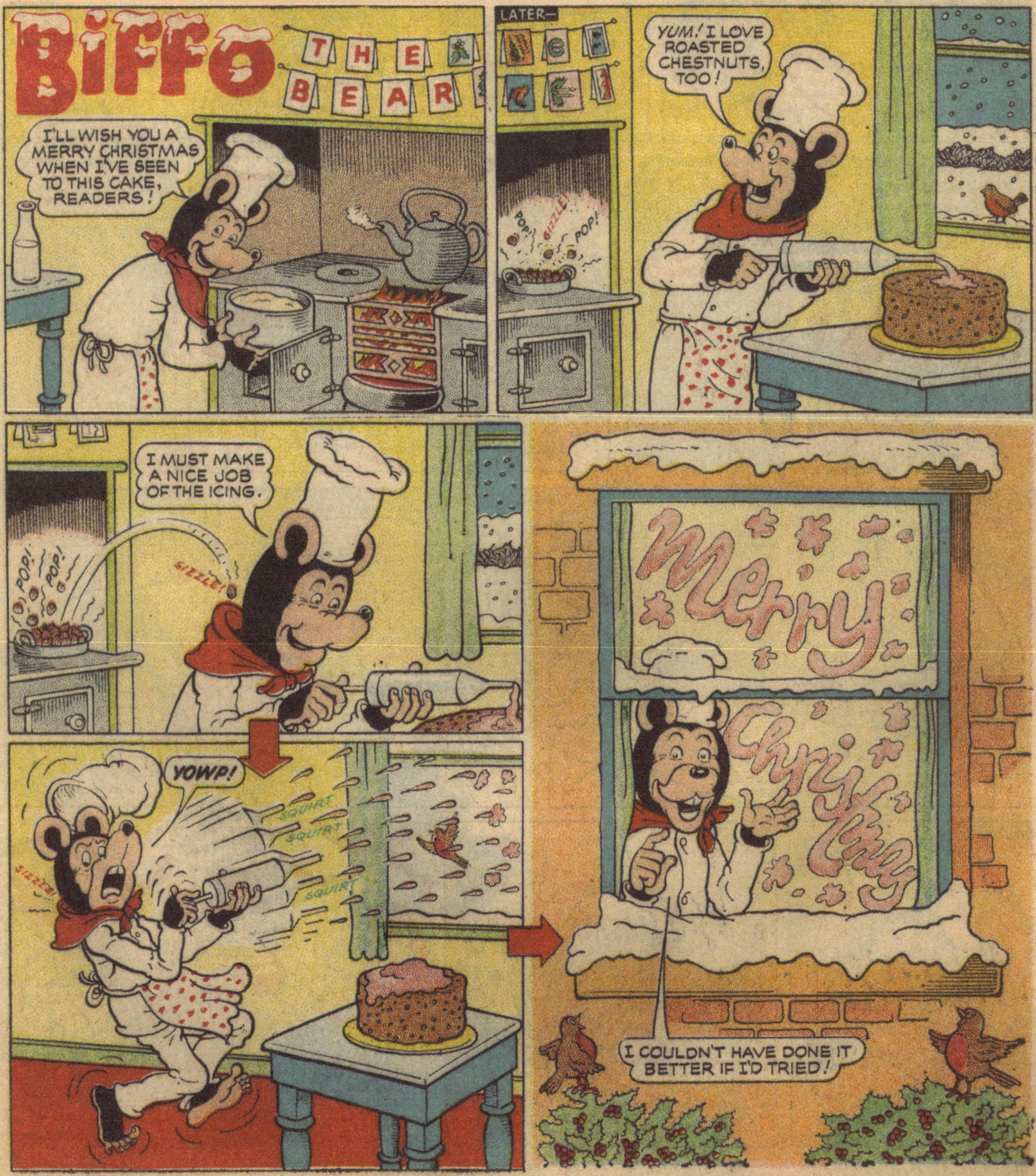

# THE BEANO

The Comic With "DENNIS the MENACE"!

No. 1638 - DEC. 8th, 1973. EVERY THURSDAY 2p

# The Christmas BEANO

No. 1640 DEC. 22nd, 1973.
EVERY THURSDAY 2p

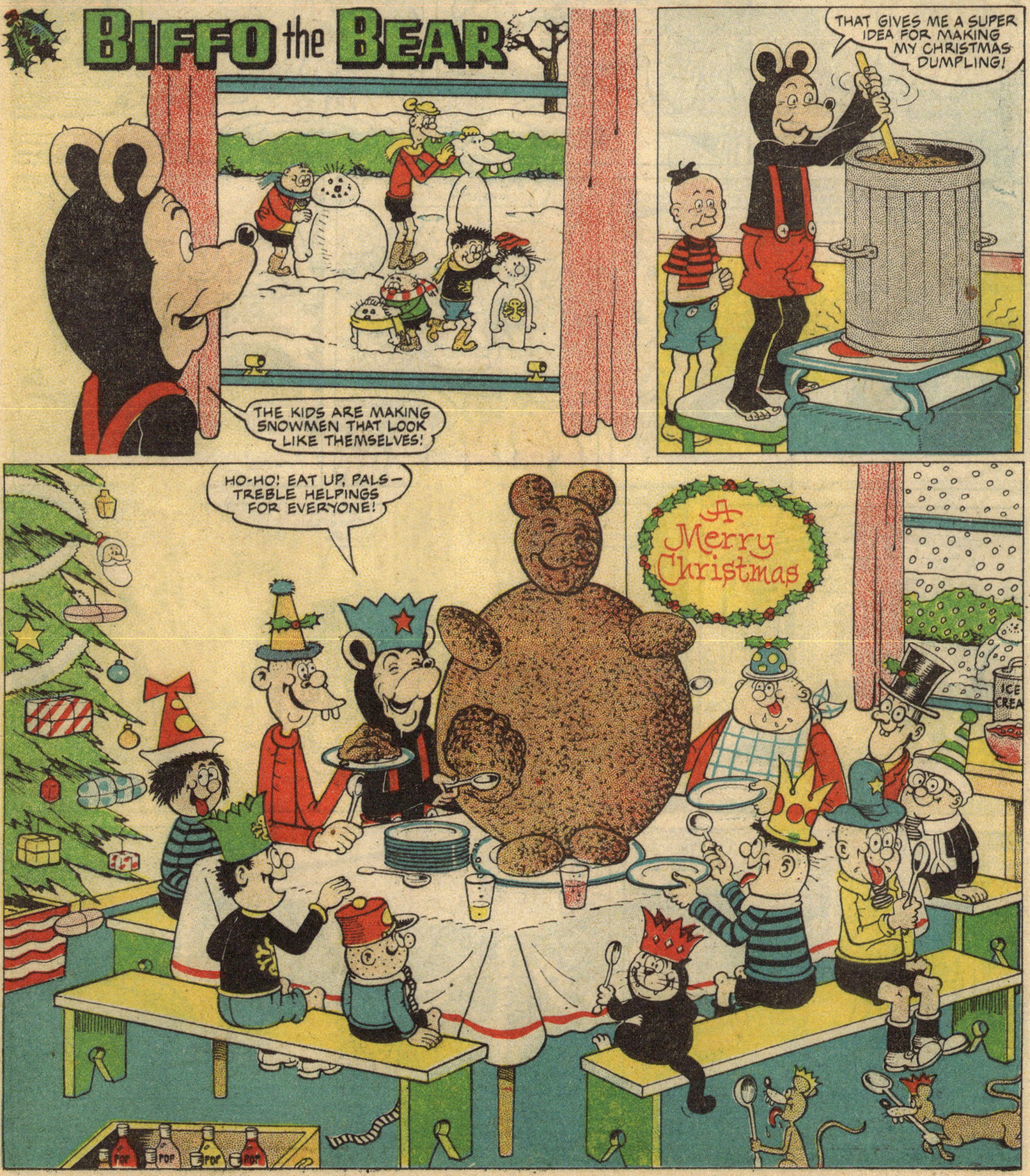

# THE BEANO

The Comic With "DENNIS the MENACE"!

No. 1648—FEB. 16th, 1974. EVERY THURSDAY 2p

FREE INSIDE—"THE HAPPY HOWLER" SIREN!

# The BEANO

No. 1678—SEP. 14th, 1974. EVERY THURSDAY 3p

# THE BEANO

The Comic With **THE BASH ST. KIDS!**

No 1683–OCT. 19th, 1974.   EVERY THURSDAY   **3p**

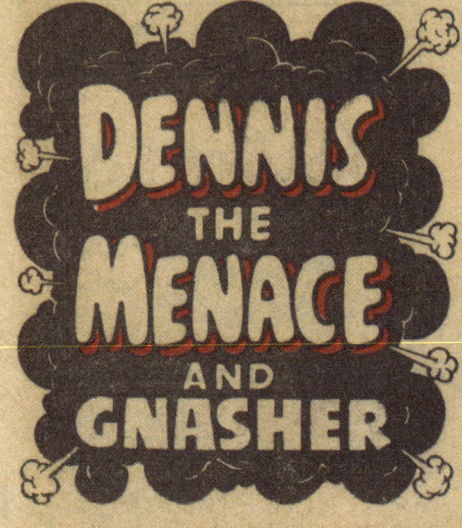

## DENNIS THE MENACE AND GNASHER

I MUST INSPECT DENNIS'S ROOM FOR TIDINESS.

DENNIS, OPEN UP!

SHOVE

HEAVE!

THIS ROOM IS LIKE A DOG'S BREAKFAST! CLEAN IT UP AT ONCE!

DOWN WITH SCHOOL

SHNAP!

MORE ON BACK PAGE

# THE BEANO CHRISTMAS

No. 1744—DEC. 20th, 1975. EVERY THURSDAY 4p

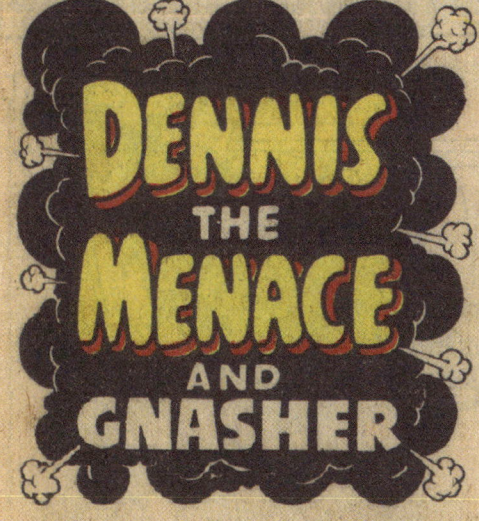

## DENNIS THE MENACE AND GNASHER

"WE'RE OFF TO GET GOODIES FOR THE SOFTIES' CHRISTMAS PARTY—"

HOPEFUL LOOKS

"—AND YOU LOT OF JOLLY ROTTERS ARE NOT BEING INVITED! YAR-BOO!"

"WE DON'T WANT TO COME TO YOUR AWFUL SOFT PARTY ANYWAY!"

— IN THE CAKE SHOP —

"OOH! TSK! HAVEN'T YOU ANYTHING LARGER?"

MERRY XMAS

"WE CAN GET ONE MADE SPECIALLY FOR YOU MADAM"

ENVIOUS

MERRY CHRISTMAS

MORE ON BACK PAGE.

THE BEANO
JOIN DENNIS'S FAN CLUB! SEE PAGE 9
DENNIS the MENACE FAN CLUB
No. 1795—DEC. 11th, 1976. EVERY THURSDAY 4p

# THE BEANO

DENNIS POSTERS TO BE WON— SEE PAGE 9

No. 1838—OCT. 8th, 1977 EVERY THURSDAY 5p

THE BEANO
FREE INSIDE A SUPER FRUITY LOLLIPOP!
No. 1892—OCT. 21st, 1978
EVERY THURSDAY
6p
DENNIS THE MENACE AND GNASHER
NOW, WHERE'S MY FREE LOLLIPOP?
FREE LOLLIPOP IN THIS WEEKS "BEANO"
OOPS!
MMM!
GNISH!
GNISH!
REMOVING WRAPPING PAPER
GNASHER!
GNICE!
CRUNCH!
BEANO
I'VE BOUGHT ANOTHER "BEANO"!
FREE LOLLIPOP IN THIS WEEKS "BEANO"
FREE LOLLIPOP IN THIS WEEKS "BEANO"
YOU'RE NOT HAVING THIS ONE, GNASHER!
BEANO
YIKES! PIEFACE!
CHOMP!
MORE ON BACK PAGE

# The BEANO

**FREE GIFT — The GNASHER GLOVE PUPPET INSIDE!**

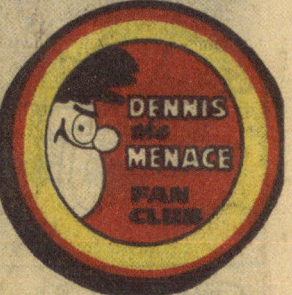

No. 1971 — APRIL 26th, 1980 • EVERY THURSDAY • 7p

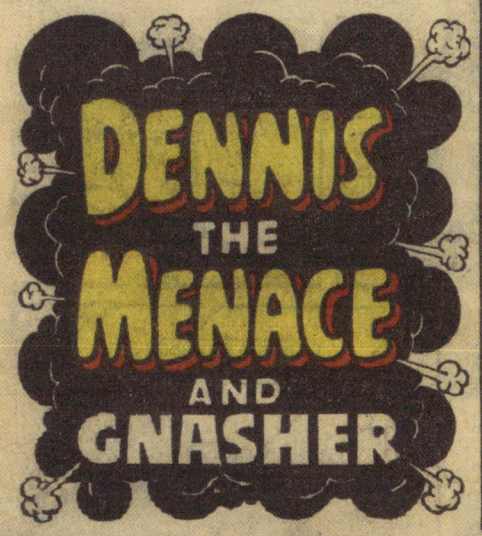

DENNIS /the/ MENACE FAN CLUB

## DENNIS THE MENACE AND GNASHER

— MINE!
GENTLE KICK

But— ERK! IT'S SLIPPED THROUGH MY HANDS!

WELL DONE! SUPER GOAL!

BETTER PUT ON MY GLOVES!

Soon— CAN I SCORE ANOTHER GOAL?

HAW-HAW! THESE ARE THE GLOVES I USED — GLOVE PUPPETS FROM OUR "BEANOS"!

EEEAAAGH!

MUMSIE!

MORE ON BACK PAGE

# № 2000 The BEANO

**with FREE COMPETITION INSIDE**

**OVER 2000 PRIZES!**

No. 2000—NOV. 15th, 1980 — EVERY THURSDAY — 8p

"HERE'S THE 2000th 'BEANO,' GNASHER!"

"AND I'LL SHOW YOU A PICTURE OF THE COVER OF THE VERY FIRST 'BEANO' ON THE BACK PAGE, READERS!"

THE BEANO
SUPER DENNIS POSTERS
TO BE WON- SEE PAGE 9.
DENNIS the MENACE FAN CLUB
No. 2046—OCT. 3rd. 1981
EVERY THURSDAY
9p
I.R. 13p (Inc. VAT)
DENNIS THE MENACE AND GNASHER
THERE'S SOMETHING MISSING TODAY SOMEHOW!
EH? THAT'S IT—
NOT WORRIED
—IT'S GNASHER! HE'S NOT THERE!
EMPTY SPACE
PHEEP!
WAH!
YIP! YAP!
WOOF!
BOW-WOW!
STILL NO GNASHER!
MORE ON BACK PAGE

# THE BEANO

WIN A DENNIS JERSEY

SEE PAGE 9

DENNIS the MENACE FAN CLUB

No. 2230 APRIL 13th, 1985 EVERY THURSDAY

14p I.R. 23p (Inc. VAT)

THE COMIC WITH IVY THE TERRIBLE

# THE BEANO

No. 2390 MAY 7th, 1988
EVERY THURSDAY
20p
I.R. 29p (inc. VAT)

# THE BEANO

**THE COMIC WITH Ivy THE TERRIBLE**

No. 2396 JUNE 18th, 1988 — EVERY THURSDAY — 20p
I.R. 29p (inc. VAT)

| WHERE'S DENNIS? | NOT PLAYING FOOTBALL | NOT DOING HOMEWORK |
|---|---|---|
| **NOT FIGHTING MINNIE** | **NOT PICKING PANSIES** | **NOT RACING BILLY WHIZZ** |
| **NOT SHARING RASHER'S SWILL** | **HERE HE IS!** | **SCARBOROUGH FESTIVAL** |

SEE THIS PAGE AS A GIANT SAND MODEL IN THE SCARBOROUGH FESTIVAL... BEING BUILT ON JUNE 16TH.

# THE BEANO

**SPECIAL 50th BIRTHDAY ISSUE**

No. 2402 JULY 30th, 1988 — EVERY THURSDAY — 20p (I.R. 29p inc VAT)

HAPPY BIRTHDAY "BEANO"

**FREE CELEBRATION POSTER INSIDE**

Original Biffo the Bear artwork for the front cover of *Beano* No. 861

Spend a LAUGH-HOUR with "The BEANO" funsters

# THE BEANO

No. 861. Jan. 17th, 1959. 2d
EVERY THURSDAY

Original Biffo the Bear artwork for the front cover of *Beano* No. 911

The BEANO, January 2, 1960

# Meet Sir Dennis Ye Menace INSIDE!

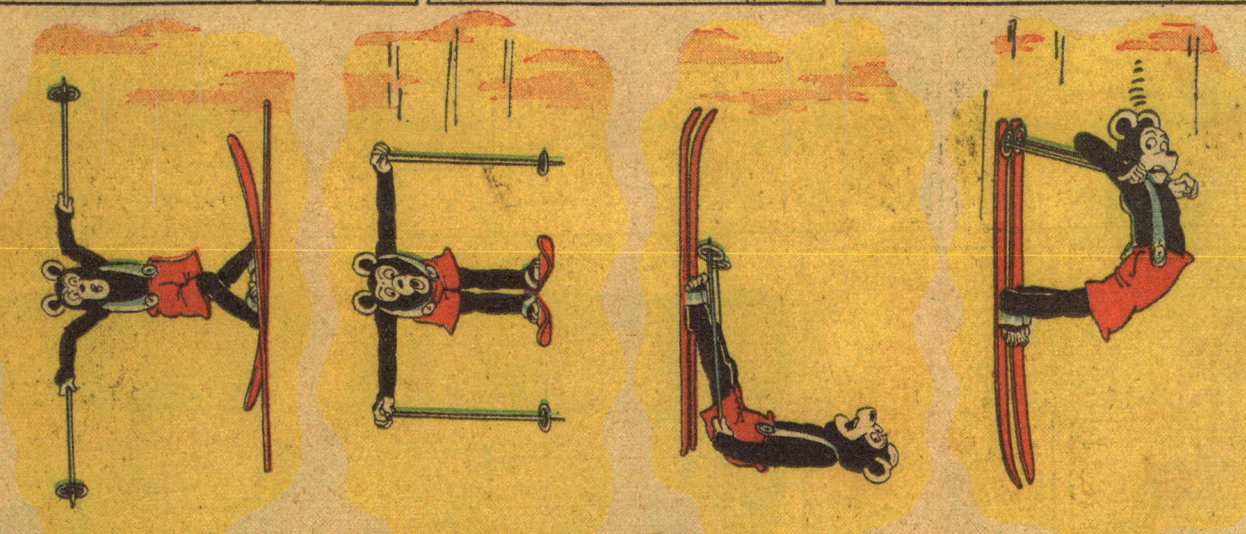

## THE BEANO

No. 911—Jan. 2nd, 1960. 2D

EVERY THURSDAY

### BIFFO the BEAR

"I MUST HAVE A SHOT AT THE SKI-JUMP!"

"HERE GOES!"

AGGH!

HELP

"WE RATHER GUESSED YOU NEEDED HELP, BIFFO!"

Original Biffo the Bear artwork for the front cover of *Beano* No. 1640

# The Christmas BEANO

No. 1640 DEC. 22nd, 1973. EVERY THURSDAY 2p

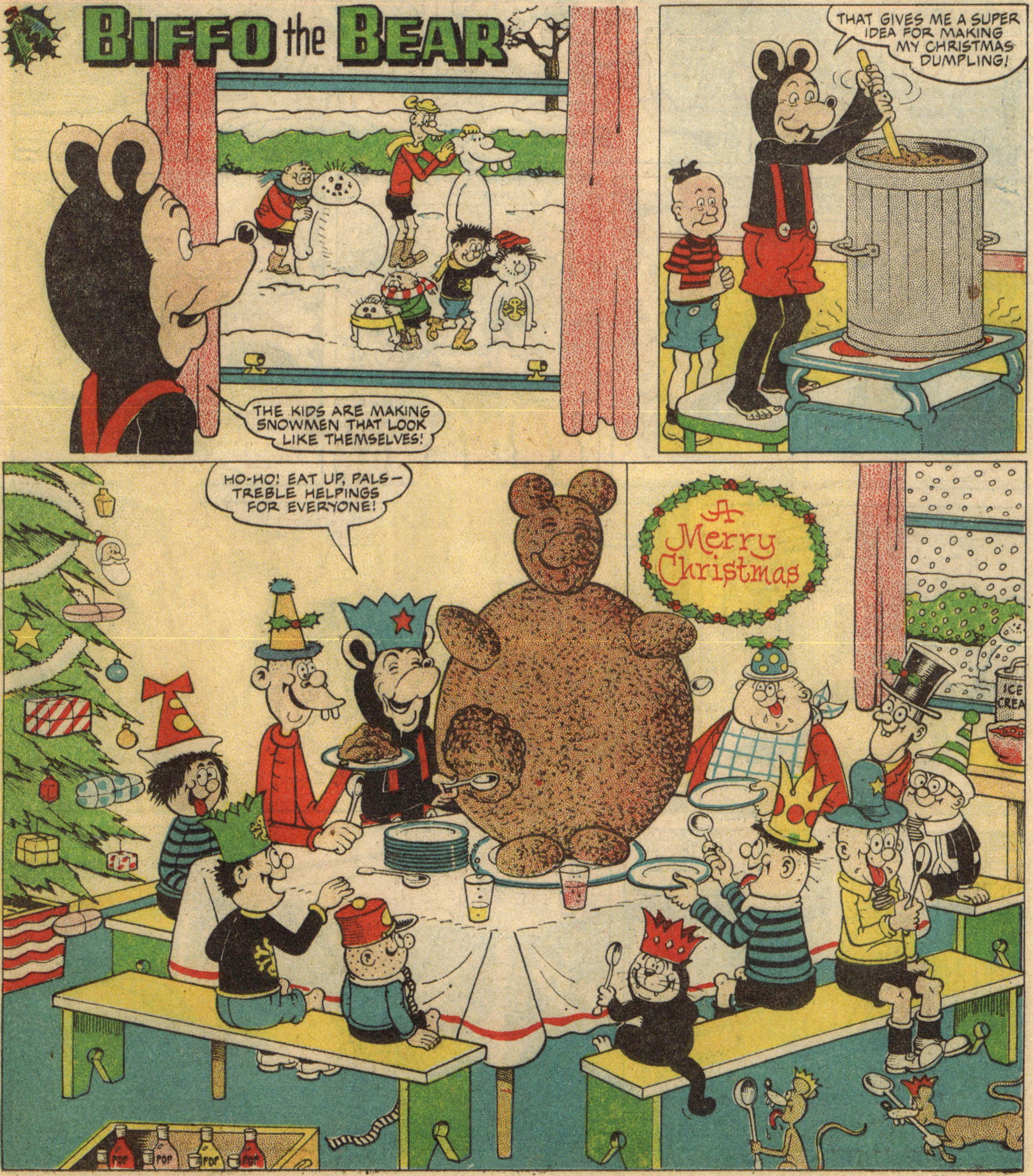

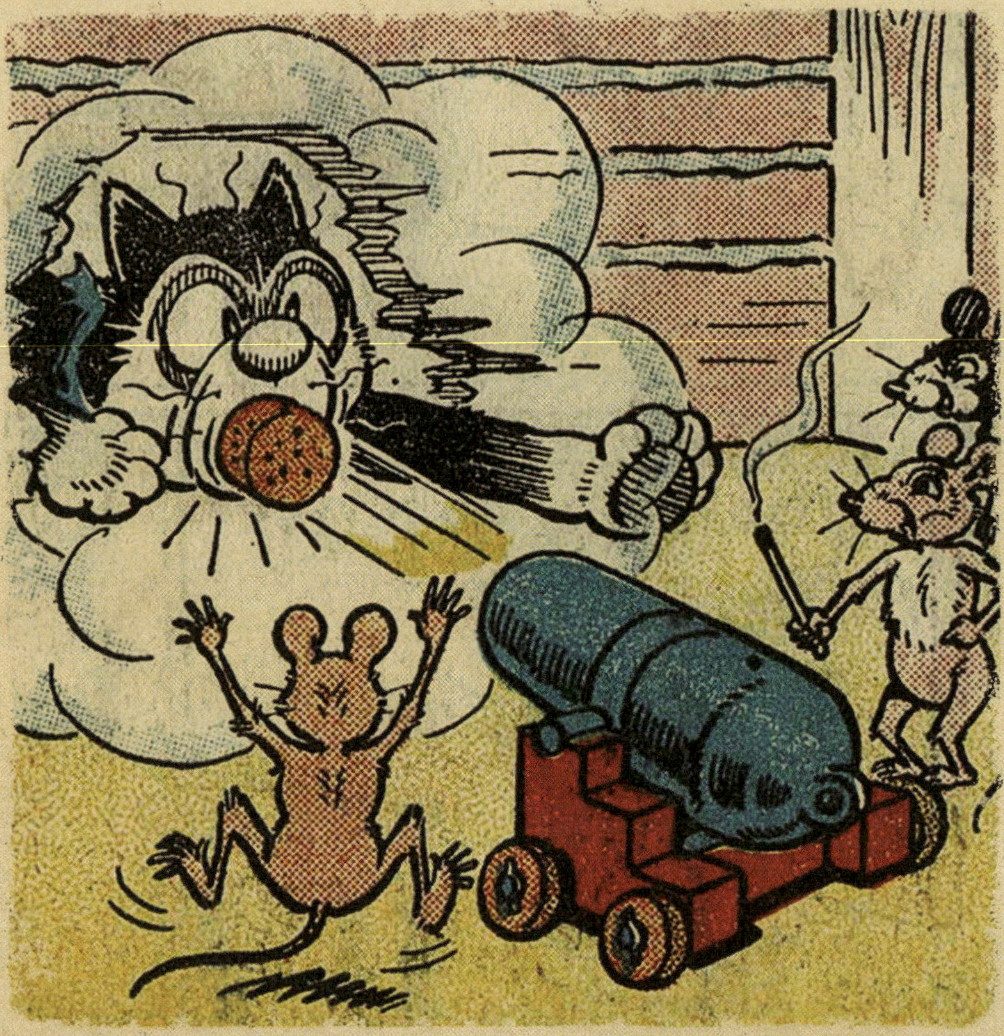

The following pages contain eighty covers of *The Dandy*, chosen for this collection, in chronological order. In addition, the original artwork for No. 2249 is shown opposite its final printed cover.

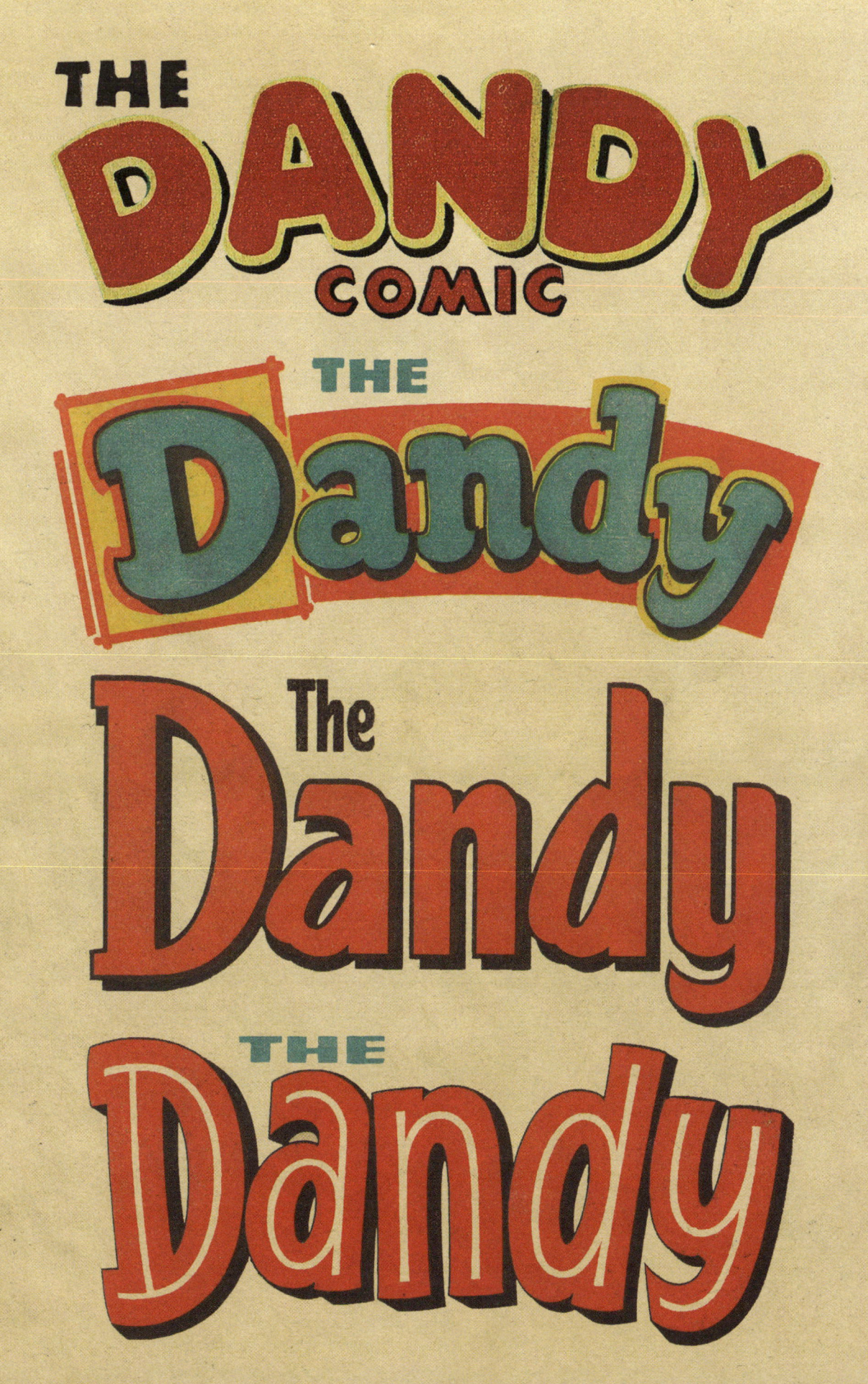

# THE DANDY COMIC

# The Dandy

# The Dandy

# THE Dandy

# THE DANDY COMIC

N° 1 DEC. 4 1937 EVERY FRIDAY 2ᵈ

## KORKY THE CAT

## N° 1 EXPRESS WHISTLER FREE INSIDE

# THE DANDY COMIC

Nº 7 · JAN. 15TH · 1938
EVERY FRIDAY
2D

## KORKY THE CAT
### IN A RAGE IN A CAGE

HELP! HELP!

# THE DANDY COMIC

Nº 49 · NOV. 5TH 1938
EVERY FRIDAY
2D

## KORKY THE CAT

Hey diddle docket,
A cat and a rocket,
Did ever you see such
a sight?
Remember, remember
The fifth of November—
The cop will remember
all right!

WHOOSH!

DAZE!

PLEASE REMEMBER THE GUY

THE DANDY COMIC
No 56 · DEC 24th 1938
EVERY FRIDAY
2d
KORKY THE CAT
THE MAYOR'S FOOTMAN TREATS KORKY ROUGH BUT KORKY MAKES OFF WITH THE MAYOR'S PLUM-DUFF!
MAYOR'S CHRISTMAS PARTY ADMISSION TICKET ONLY
ADMIT ONE
ADMIT ONE
BACK DOOR
FOR MAYOR'S XMAS PARTY
FOR MAYOR'S XMAS PARTY
BANG!
HI! COME BACK!
WAY OUT

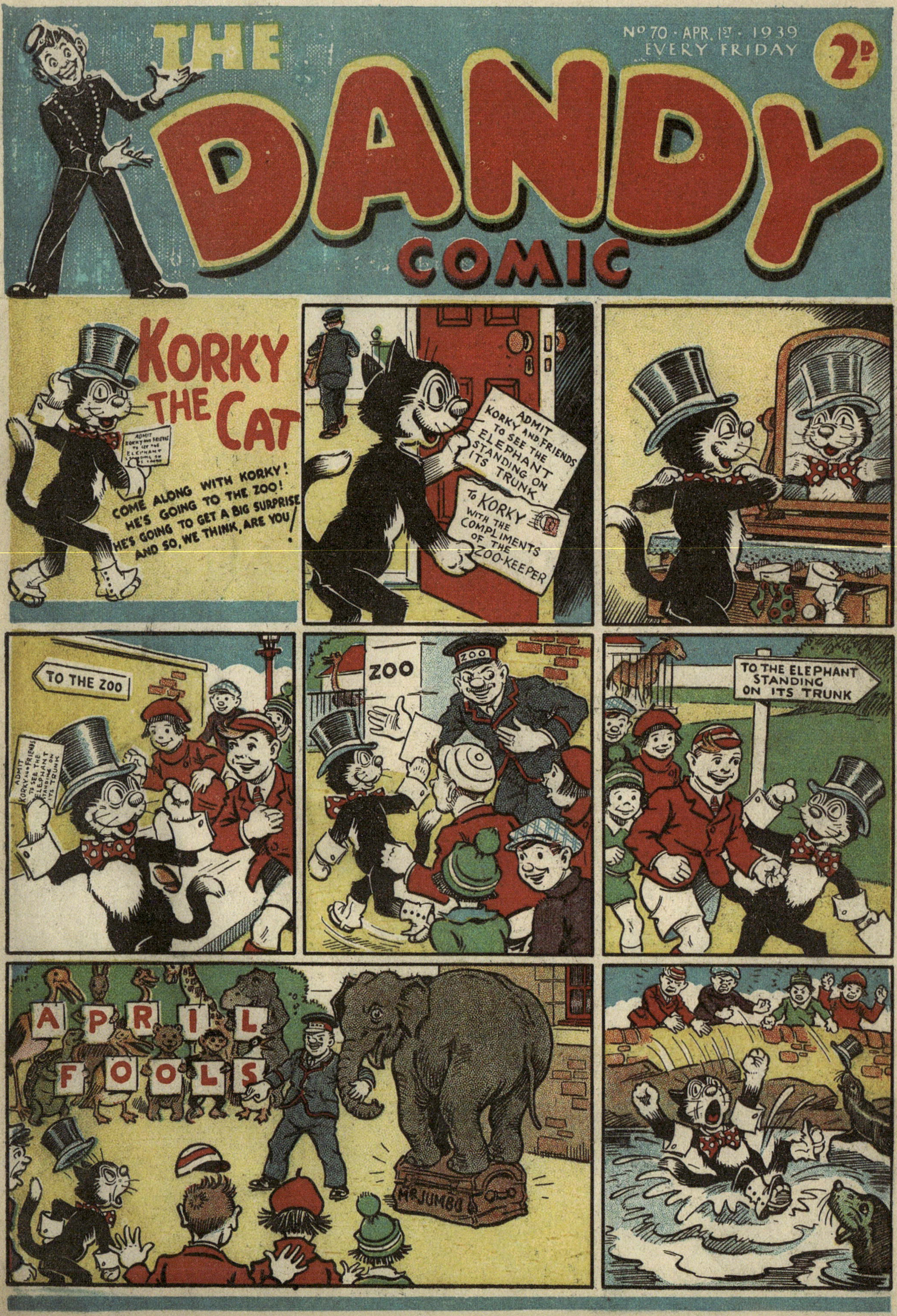
THE DANDY COMIC
Nº 70 · APR. 1ST · 1939
EVERY FRIDAY
2D
KORKY THE CAT
COME ALONG WITH KORKY! HE'S GOING TO THE ZOO! HE'S GOING TO GET A BIG SURPRISE AND SO, WE THINK, ARE YOU!
ADMIT KORKY AND FRIENDS TO SEE THE ELEPHANT STANDING ON ITS TRUNK.
TO KORKY WITH THE COMPLIMENTS OF THE ZOO-KEEPER
TO THE ZOO
ZOO
ZOO
TO THE ELEPHANT STANDING ON ITS TRUNK
APRIL FOOLS
MR JUMBO

# THE DANDY COMIC

No 71 · APR. 8TH · 1939
EVERY FRIDAY
2D

## Korky the Cat

When the egg was opened the mice began to sing, "Ha, ha, Korky, what a joke! And does your poor nose sting?"

A Happy Easter to Korky

BONG!

REVENGE!

SNIFF

EEK! EEK! EEK!

EEK!

BEWARE OF THE ROCKS

THE DANDY COMIC
No101 NOV. 4TH 1939
EVERY FRIDAY
2D
KORKY THE CAT
A SPECIAL COP SAYS, "NO FIREWORKS ALLOWED".
BUT KORKY'S NOT WORRIED A BIT.
FOR WHEN HE HAS GOT HIS CUNNING REVENGE
THAT COPPER IS LIKE ADOLF HIT!
PASTE
SPECIAL COP
GUY FAWKES' DAY
NO FIREWORKS ALLOWED
BY ORDER OF THE POLICE
PASTE
GUY FAWKES' DAY
KORKY'S GRAND DISPLAY OF FIREWORKS
COME AND SEE HUNDREDS OF STARS
ENTRANCE
NOW I'LL FIX HIS HAIR AND STICK ON THIS MOUSTACHE.
LOOK! HE THINKS HE'S HITLER!
SPECIAL COP
THAT'LL TEACH HIM!
AMBULANCE
DRINK, HORSEY DRINK

**NUTTY NOUGAT BAR — FREE INSIDE**

# THE DANDY COMIC

N° 121. MAR. 23RD 1940 — EVERY FRIDAY — 2D

## KORKY the CAT

HUMPTY-DUMPTY IS KORKY THE CAT,
HUMPTY-DUMPTY SQUASHES HENS FLAT,
AND ALL THE TOWN'S JUDGES, AND ALL THE TOWNSFOLK
CHEER KORKY'S CARRIAGE WITH HENS IN THE YOKE!

# THE DANDY COMIC

**THIS ISSUE IS PACKED WITH EASTER AND APRIL FIRST FUN!**

Nº 211  APRIL 4TH 1942  2D

## KORKY THE CAT

JUST LOOK BELOW AND THEN YOU'LL SEE MICE MAKE KORK AN APRIL FOOL. WILL KORKY'S SMOKE CLOUDS BEAT THEM YET? OH NO! THE FIREMAN LEAVES HIM WET!

**EASTER FUN FOR EVERYONE!**

# THE DANDY COMIC

No 238 APRIL 17TH 1943 — 2D

## KORKY the CAT

*Korky's eggs are made of wood, and as a shield, one proves good. But their uses don't stop there, for with them, Korky starts a fair!*

1. "Deliver these wooden eggs to Scottie, the confectioner!"
2. *(Korky wheels the cart of eggs away)*
3. PING! OW!
4. KLONK — HA! HA!
5. CRACK!
6. "I can't use these eggs; they're all scratched and dirty!"
7. IDEA
8. **KORKY'S OWN EASTER FUN FAIR** — WATER CHUTE — CASH — PAY HERE

MAY DAY FUN WITH KORKY!
THE DANDY COMIC
No239 MAY 1st 1943
2d
KORKY THE CAT
SEE HOW THE KITTENS CALMLY STOLE, KORKY'S BLIND AND BARBER'S POLE. THEY USED THEM FOR THEIR MAY DAY DANCE AND ROUND POOR KORKY THEY DID PRANCE!
KORKY, HAIRDRESSER
SLAM!
SHAVING
NEXT MORNING
DERE UNCLE KORKY WILL YOU PLESE CUM AND PLAY THE MUSIK AT OUR MAYPOLE DANCE TO-MORROW? YOUR LOVING NEPHEWS THE KITTENS
TO UNCLE KORKY
R-R-RIP
HO! HO! HO!
SHAVING

**GRAND NEW STORY STARTS INSIDE!**

# THE DANDY COMIC

No. 250—OCT. 2nd, 1943      2ᴅ

## Korky the Cat

THE KITS REFUSE TO HAVE THEIR BATH, AND ROUSE POOR KORKY'S WRATH. BUT WITH A BRUSH AND A POT OF GLUE, HE GIVES THEM A BATH AND A SEE-SAW TOO!

1. COME AND GET YOUR BATH, KITS! — NO! WE WANT TO SEE-SAW!
2. IDEA
3. (Korky runs with glue pot)
4. (Korky glues the plank)
5. **SPECIAL 250TH NUMBER**
6. COME ON, KITS, GET ON THE OTHER END AND HAVE A SEE-SAW WITH ME!
7. HELP! WE'RE STUCK!
8. (see-saw action)
9. (splash finale)

**NEW FUN AND ADVENTURE STORY : HAPPY-GO-LUCKY : BEGINS TODAY**

# THE DANDY COMIC

No. 290—APR. 14th, 1945   2d

## KORKY the CAT

*"Bring that mutton chop back!"* you can hear the butcher growl. But the snarling face in the mirror made him far too scared to howl!

Panel 1: "Mutton! Mutton! I told you not to send mutton!"

Panel 3: "Stop thief! Bring back that chop!"

Panel 4: HALL OF MIRRORS — COME IN AND SEE HOW QUEER YOU LOOK IN OUR FUNNY MIRRORS

Panel 8: WAY OUT →

**WHERE'S KORKY THIS WEEK?** SEE HIM ON THE BACK PAGE.

# THE DANDY COMIC

No. 295—JUNE 23rd, 1945 — 2d

## Keyhole Kate

*Keyholes on the mantelpiece, keyholes on the floor, keyholes everywhere you look — but not on Katie's door!*

**Panel 1:** "We'll have to get Kate's room re-decorated!"

**Panel 2:** "Let me do it in my own way Mum!"

**Panel 3:** SALE

**Panel 4:** (Kate with pickaxe)

**Panel 5:** (brick hits man)

**Panel 6:** "Come up and see what I've done!"

**Panel 7:** "There!"

**Panel 8:** (bedroom with keyhole-shaped mirror, fireplace and window)

**Panel 9:** "But there's no keyhole in the door!"

**Panel 10:** "No fear! Nobody's going to peep into my room!"

THE DANDY Comic    January 5, 1946.

HAPPY NEW YEAR

FROM KORKY TO HIS PALS

## 1946 · KORKY'S CALENDAR · 1946

| JANUARY | FEBRUARY | MARCH | APRIL |
|---|---|---|---|
| S  -  6 13 20 27 | S  -  3 10 17 24 | S  -  3 10 17 24 31 | S  -  7 14 21 28 |
| M  -  7 14 21 28 | M  -  4 11 18 25 | M  -  4 11 18 25  - | M  1  8 15 22 29 |
| Tu 1  8 15 22 29 | Tu -  5 12 19 26 | Tu -  5 12 19 26  - | Tu 2  9 16 23 30 |
| W  2  9 16 23 30 | W  -  6 13 20 27 | W  -  6 13 20 27  - | W  3 10 17 24  - |
| Th 3 10 17 24 31 | Th -  7 14 21 28 | Th -  7 14 21 28  - | Th 4 11 18 25  - |
| F  4 11 18 25  - | F  1  8 15 22  - | F  1  8 15 22 29  - | F  5 12 19 26  - |
| S  5 12 19 26  - | S  2  9 16 23  - | S  2  9 16 23 30  - | S  6 13 20 27  - |

| MAY | JUNE | JULY | AUGUST |
|---|---|---|---|
| S  -  5 12 19 26 | S  -  2  9 16 23 30 | S  -  7 14 21 28 | S  -  4 11 18 25 |
| M  -  6 13 20 27 | M  -  3 10 17 24  - | M  1  8 15 22 29 | M  -  5 12 19 26 |
| Tu -  7 14 21 28 | Tu -  4 11 18 25  - | Tu 2  9 16 23 30 | Tu -  6 13 20 27 |
| W  1  8 15 22 29 | W  -  5 12 19 26  - | W  3 10 17 24 31 | W  -  7 14 21 28 |
| Th 2  9 16 23 30 | Th -  6 13 20 27  - | Th 4 11 18 25  - | Th 1  8 15 22 29 |
| F  3 10 17 24 31 | F  -  7 14 21 28  - | F  5 12 19 26  - | F  2  9 16 23 30 |
| S  4 11 18 25  - | S  1  8 15 22 29  - | S  6 13 20 27  - | S  3 10 17 24 31 |

| SEPTEMBER | OCTOBER | NOVEMBER | DECEMBER |
|---|---|---|---|
| S  1  8 15 22 29 | S  -  6 13 20 27 | S  -  3 10 17 24 | S  1  8 15 22 29 |
| M  2  9 16 23 30 | M  -  7 14 21 28 | M  -  4 11 18 25 | M  2  9 16 23 30 |
| Tu 3 10 17 24  - | Tu 1  8 15 22 29 | Tu -  5 12 19 26 | Tu 3 10 17 24 31 |
| W  4 11 18 25  - | W  2  9 16 23 30 | W  -  6 13 20 27 | W  4 11 18 25  - |
| Th 5 12 19 26  - | Th 3 10 17 24 31 | Th -  7 14 21 28 | Th 5 12 19 26  - |
| F  6 13 20 27  - | F  4 11 18 25  - | F  1  8 15 22 29 | F  6 13 20 27  - |
| S  7 14 21 28  - | S  5 12 19 26  - | S  2  9 16 23 30 | S  7 14 21 28  - |

← CUT ROUND OUTLINE    CUT ROUND OUTLINE →

PRINTED AND PUBLISHED IN GREAT BRITAIN BY D. C. THOMSON & CO., LTD., 12 FETTER LANE, FLEET STREET, LONDON, E.C.4.
REGISTERED FOR TRANSMISSION BY CANADIAN MAGAZINE POST.

# FIREWORKS FUN FOR EVERYONE

## THE DANDY COMIC
No. 331—NOV. 9th, 1946 — 2D

### KORKY the CAT

EENY, MEENY, MINEY, MO,
A MOUSE HITS KORKY ON THE TOE.
HE GIVES A HOLLER, LETS MATCH GO —
AND THAT'S WHAT STARTS A FIREWORK SHOW!

THAT NIGHT

OUGH!

BANG!!

BUMPER XMAS NUMBER

ALL YOUR COMIC PALS ARE HERE — TO FILL YOU FULL OF XMAS CHEER!

No. 334—DEC. 21st, 1946.

2d

# THE DANDY COMIC

## KORKY THE CAT

YOUR DANDY CHUMS ALL RAISE A CHEER —
THEY'RE MERRY, BRIGHT AND HEARTY,
BECAUSE THERE'S DUFF AND GINGER BEER
AT KORKY'S CHRISTMAS PARTY.

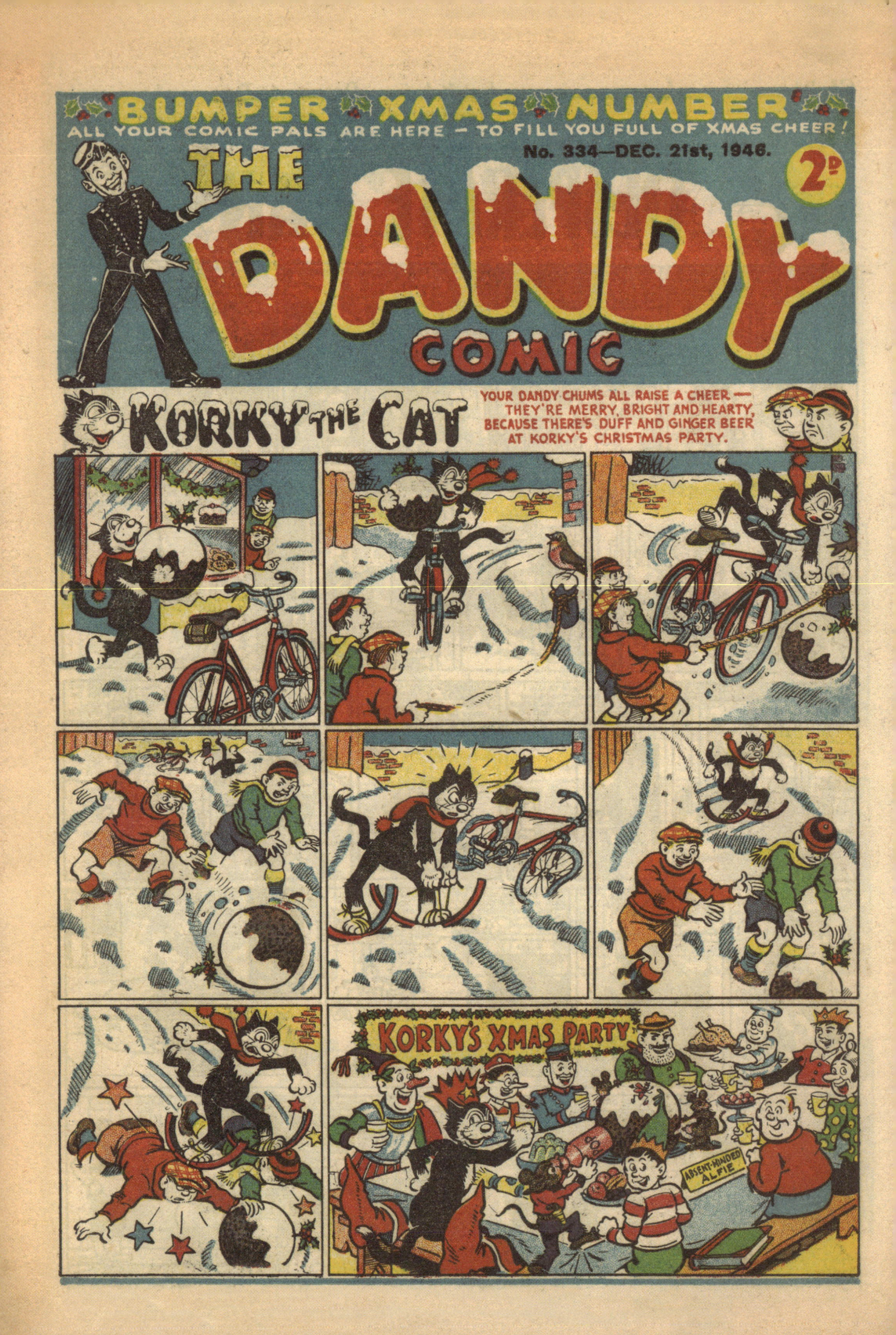

**HURRAY, HURRAY FOR GUY FAWKES DAY!** All the fireworks fun inside.

# THE DANDY COMIC

No. 356—NOV. 8th, 1947       2D

## KORKY THE CAT

REMEMBER, REMEMBER THE FIFTH OF NOVEMBER— BUT YOU CAN SAFELY BET THAT'S NOW A DATE THAT KORKY WILL ALWAYS WANT TO FORGET!

**BIG BONEHEAD, THE ZULU WARRIOR COMES TO BRITAIN** — SEE THE GREAT NEW STORY INSIDE

# THE DANDY COMIC

No. 369 — MAY 8th, 1948    2d

## KORKY the CAT

KORKY SMOKES THE MICE OUT, BUT THE MICE HAVE GOT A TRICK THAT SCALPS POOR OLD MA MURPHY AND UN-WHISKERS WHISKERY DICK!

1. Oh boy, these are lovely cigars — I must invite some of my "Dandy" pals round to a smoking party.

2. (Korky writing invitations)

3. (Guests arrive)

4. He'll never know we've swopped them.

5. Now you must try my cigars.

6. BANG! BANG! BANG! BANG!

7. (The aftermath)

8. Coo! Look at Whiskery Dick — he's got no whiskers. And Ma Murphy has lost her wig.

NEW THRILL STORY IN THIS FIREWORKS NUMBER
LOOK INSIDE FOR "THE CROAKER HOLDS THE CLUE"
No. 382—NOV. 6th, 1948
THE DANDY COMIC
2d
KORKY THE CAT
THE MICE MIX POWDER IN A BOWL.
KORKY WONDERS WHAT—AND WHY?
HE SOON FINDS OUT JUST WHAT, POOR SOUL!
AND THAT IS WHY HE'S NOW THE GUY!
NO FIREWORKS
HERE COMES KORKY! SCRAM!
WHAT HAVE THEY BEEN MAKING? PHEW! WHAT A SMELL!
BANG!
HA-HA! HE DIDN'T KNOW THAT WAS A FIREWORKS MIXTURE!
HELP THE GUY

GRAND XMAS NUMBER
WITH XMAS THRILLS AND LAUGHTER TOO,
AND LOADS OF XMAS CHEER FOR YOU.
THE DANDY COMIC
No. 385—DEC. 18th, 1948
2d
KORKY THE CAT
PAT A KAKE, PAT A KAKE, BAKER MAN
JAPED POOR OLD KORKY WITH HIS VAN,
BUT KORKY'S TRICK WITH A BIG SNOWBALL
BRINGS A MERRY XMAS TO THE KITTENS AND ALL
HONK! HONK!
HAW-HAW!
PAT A KAKE BAKER
KORKY
A MERRY CHRISTMAS FROM KORKY AND THE KITS
POP

HIS MAJESTY'S WIZARD **Mr G. WHIZZ** IS IN THE GREAT NEW LAUGH STORY INSIDE.

# THE DANDY COMIC

No. 393 — APRIL 9th, 1949  2ᴅ

## KORKY the CAT

HIS EASTER EGG IS FULL OF JOKES SO KORKY THINKS IT'S JUST A HOAX. BUT ONCE IT'S WRECKED HE FINDS IT'S NOT AS BAD AN EGG AS HE FIRST THOUGHT.

HA-HA! THERE WERE GOOD THINGS IN IT AFTER ALL!

GREAT NEWS FOR EVERY BOY AND GIRL INSIDE
THE DANDY COMIC
No. 395—MAY 7th, 1949
2d
KORKY THE CAT
HERE'S A RAILWAY TUNNEL WHERE IT'S BLACK AS NIGHT— THE VERY PLACE FOR KORKY TO HAVE AN APPETITE!
HUNGER
THIRD 1357
KEEP AWAY, YOU!
WOW!
SEE WHAT I CAUGHT
THAT'S NOTHING! SEE WHAT I CAUGHT!
MINE IS A LOT BIGGER THAN YOURS.
OH, NO IT ISN'T! JUST WAIT TILL THE TRAIN GETS OUT OF THIS TUNNEL. THEN WE'LL SEE.

BUMPER FIREWORKS NUMBER
WITH AN EXCITING NEW
BLACK BOB
STORY STARTING INSIDE
No. 415—NOV. 5th, 1949
EVERY TUESDAY
2D
THE DANDY COMIC
KORKY THE CAT
HERE'S A TOUGH-GUY COPPER WHO CHASES KORKY CAT. THAT COPPER NOW'S A TOPPER OF A GUY IN KORKY'S CART!
COME BACK WITH THOSE ROCKETS. NO FIREWORKS ALLOWED ON MY BEAT!
SHOOSH!
YOU GET MY HELMET BACK!
I'LL FIX HIM!
BANG!
WE'VE GOT A "COPPER" FOR THE GUY

# THE DANDY COMIC

**THE RETURN OF DANNY LONGLEGS** • **SEE THE GREAT NEWS IN THIS** — **BUMPER EASTER NUMBER**

No. 437 — APRIL 8th, 1950 — EVERY TUESDAY — 2ᵈ

## KORKY THE CAT

IT'S A HAPPY EASTER, KORKY! BUT JUST BECAUSE YOU'RE CUTE, FOR THOUGH THE MICE HAVE TRICKED YOU, IT'S THEY WHO RUN — HOT FOOT!

- TO KORKY WITH LOVE
- IDEA
- LATER
- I SMELL CHEESE, BOYS — IT'S IN THE EGG!
- GR-R-R
- I'M GOING TO HAVE A HAPPY EASTER WITHOUT THEM.

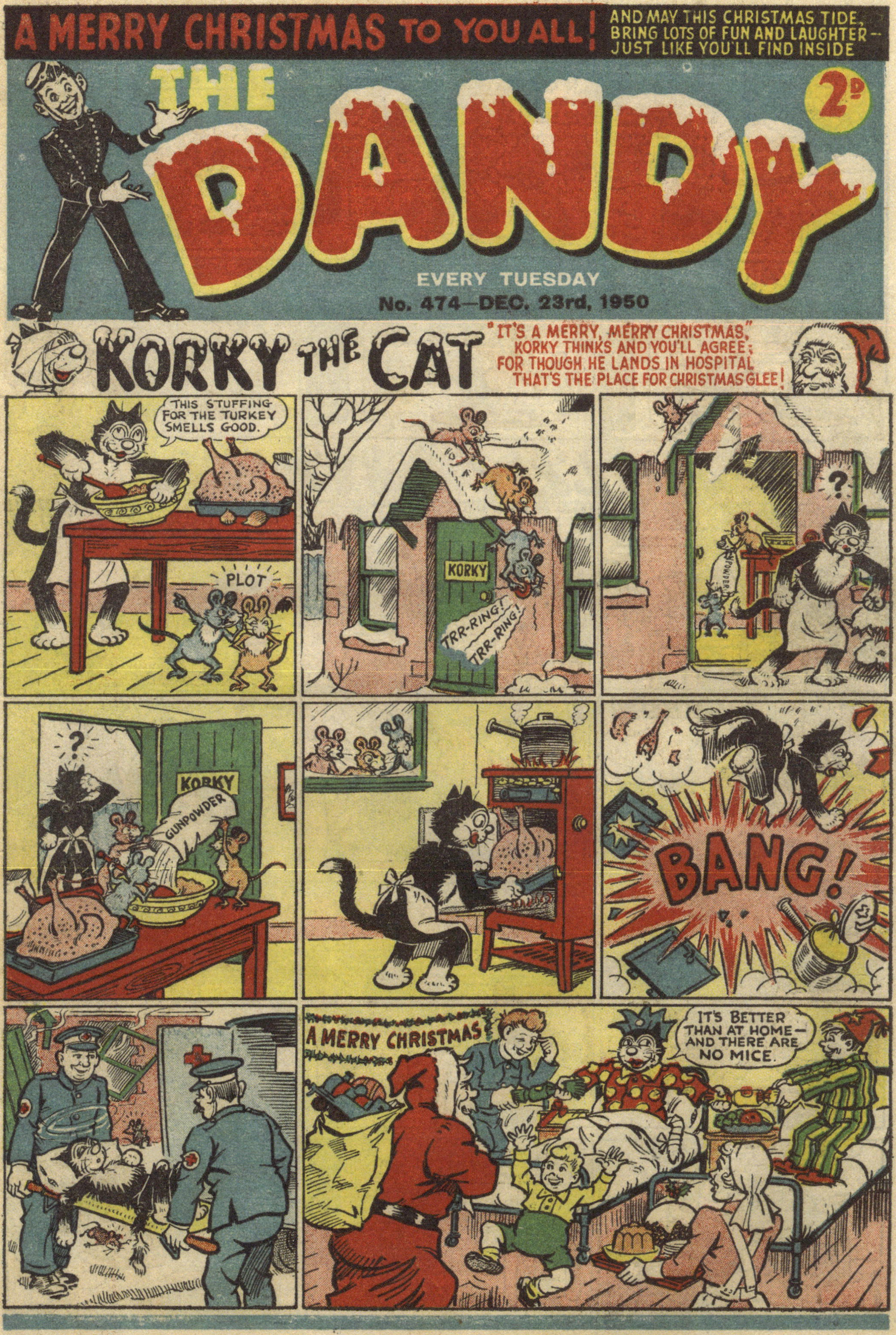
A MERRY CHRISTMAS TO YOU ALL!
AND MAY THIS CHRISTMAS TIDE, BRING LOTS OF FUN AND LAUGHTER— JUST LIKE YOU'LL FIND INSIDE
THE DANDY
2D
EVERY TUESDAY
No. 474—DEC. 23rd, 1950
KORKY THE CAT
"IT'S A MERRY, MERRY CHRISTMAS," KORKY THINKS AND YOU'LL AGREE; FOR THOUGH HE LANDS IN HOSPITAL THAT'S THE PLACE FOR CHRISTMAS GLEE!
THIS STUFFING FOR THE TURKEY SMELLS GOOD.
PLOT
KORKY
TRR-RING! TRR-RING!
?
GUNPOWDER
?
KORKY
GUNPOWDER
BANG!
A MERRY CHRISTMAS
IT'S BETTER THAN AT HOME— AND THERE ARE NO MICE.

GREAT NEWS INSIDE ABOUT **A NEW KIND OF STORY WITH NEW KINDS OF THRILLS**

# THE DANDY
**2ᴅ**

EVERY TUESDAY
No. 494—MAY 12th, 1951

## KORKY the CAT

CUTE KORKY HAS A PLAN, AND IT'S ONE THAT CAN STOP MICE FROM BEING SUCH PESTS; BUT HIS WALL IS SMASHED AND KORKY BASHED! FOR ONCE THE MICE BEAT HIM AT JESTS!

1. *(Korky sees mice)*
2. "GOSH! LOOK AT THE SIZE OF THE HOLE THEY'VE MADE — I MUST CLOSE IT UP."
3. "AH! HERE'S WHAT I WANT." — HOUSEHOLD CEMENT / ALPHABET BLOCKS
4. *(Korky building wall)*
5. "THAT'LL FIX THE MICE!" — NO ROAD THIS WAY
6. INSIDE THE MOUSE-HOLE — KORKY'S HOME — KEEP OUT
7. KORKY'S HOME — KEEP OUT *(mice light a rocket)*
8. *(explosion)*
9. "HA-HA-HA!" — DOWN WITH KORKY

**GREAT NEW BLACK BOB STORY IN THIS BIG FIREWORKS NUMBER**

# THE DANDY

2ᴅ

EVERY TUESDAY
No. 519—NOV. 3rd, 1951

## KORKY THE CAT

CRACK—BANG! GOES KORKY'S TAIL; HIS MONSTER NOSE GLOWS BRIGHT. HE THOUGHT 'TWAS FUN TO SCARE THE KITTS— BUT IT'S HE WHO GETS THE FRIGHT!

- More fireworks for Guy Fawkes Day, Uncle Korky.
- I'll give the kittens a scare.
- Wow! It's a monster!
- Ha-ha-ha!
- Bah! It's only Uncle Korky!
- That was funny, Uncle Korky. Let's see you scare old Giles.
- Quick! Turn the handle!

CHRISTMAS FUN NUMBER

# THE DANDY

2d

EVERY TUESDAY

No. 527—DEC. 29th, 1951

## KORKY THE CAT

A BAR OF SOAP WRECKED KORKY'S HOPE
AND BROUGHT OUR CAT TO TEARS.
BUT HEAPS OF TOYS CHANGED TEARS TO JOYS—
IT'S THE MERRIEST XMAS FOR YEARS!

# THE DANDY

**A HAPPY NEW YEAR says BARNEY'S BEAR**

2ᴰ

EVERY TUESDAY
No. 580—JAN. 3rd, 1953

## KORKY the CAT

WHEN THE MICE WON'T SPEAK TO KORKY, KORKY MAKES THINGS HUM; BUT THE MICE BRING UP ARTILLERY AND STRIKE POOR KORKY DUMB!

**Panel 1:** I resolve to be friendly with all MICE signed Korky

**Panel 2:** I'LL SUCK THE MICE FROM THEIR HOLES SO THAT I CAN TELL THEM WE'RE TO BE FRIENDS.

**Panel 3:** INSIDE THE HOLE — HOLD ON, BOYS— THIS BANGER WILL STOP HIM SUCKING US OUT.

**Panel 4:** BANG!

**Panel 5:** I'LL GO IN MYSELF AND TALK TO THEM.

**Panel 6:** NO! NO!

**Panel 7:** (smoke)

**Panel 8:** MM-M-M! MEANING— BRING BACK THAT BLINKING CORKSCREW! — HAPPY NEW YEAR, KORKY!

**YOUR CORONATION HOLIDAY PAPER**

# THE DANDY

2ᴰ

EVERY TUESDAY
No. 602—JUNE 6th, 1953.

## KORKY the CAT

"KORKY CAT, KORKY CAT, WHERE HAVE YOU BEEN?"
"I'VE BEEN TO LONDON TO SEE THE QUEEN."
"KORKY CAT, KORKY CAT, WHAT DID YOU THERE?"
"I CHEERED HER AND CHEERED HER FROM UP IN THE AIR."

I KNOW HOW I CAN SEE THE CORONATION PROCESSION.

# THE DANDY

**FIREWORKS FUN IN THE WILD WEST** — SEE DESPERATE DAN

2ᴅ

Every Tuesday. No. 624—NOV. 7th. 1953.

## KORKY the CAT

THE FIREWORKS DEALER WAS A MISER — HE'S NOW A POORER MAN, BUT WISER, AS ALL HIS PROFIT DISAPPEARS IN THE BEST **FREE** GUY FAWKES SHOW FOR YEARS!

1. "Can we have a shilling's worth of fireworks, boss?" — "No, I'm storing them in the old warehouse to get a big price on the 'Fifth'."

2. WAREHOUSE

3. (Carrying gunpowder)

4. "Let's sweep up that powder and make our own fireworks." — "No, give me a match!"

5. (Explosion)

6. (Fireworks display at the warehouse)

FIREWORKS FUN
AND A GREAT NEW PAL
ANGEL FACE
THE DANDY
2d
EVERY TUESDAY
No. 676—NOV. 6th, 1954.
KORKY THE CAT
WHEN KORKY HAS HIS LITTLE JOKE, THE MICE WANT TIT-FOR-TAT. SO A BOX OF SQUIBS GOES UP IN SMOKE— AND SO DOES KORKY CAT!
THIS IS FIREWORKS DAY.
AND I WANT THE MICE TO SEE MY FIREWORKS DISPLAY!
BANG!
BANG!
HO-HO! I'VE MADE A CATCH!
LATER
SOAK HIM WITH PETROL.
PETROL
FIREWORKS
MATCHES
MATCHES FOR DRUMSTICKS—
?
—AND OFF HE MARCHES.
OH, NO!
BANG!
HA-HA-HA!

# THE DANDY

**XMAS FUN AND GREAT XMAS NEWS INSIDE**

2ᴅ

EVERY TUESDAY
No. 683—DEC. 25th, 1954.

## KORKY THE CAT

THERE ARE SANTAS TALL AND SANTAS SMALL AND SANTAS THIN AND FAT.
BUT NEVER TILL NOW, WITH A MERRY MIAOW—
A SANTA KORKY CAT!

THE FISHERMEN'S XMAS TREAT NO CATS

"YOU'RE TOO EARLY — AND ANYWAY NO CATS!"

"HA-HA! WHAT A FUNNY LITTLE SANTA CLAUS! IN YOU GO AND WAIT FOR THE PARTY TO BEGIN."

"A MERRY CHRISTMAS, EVERYBODY!"

# A THRILLING NEW YEAR!

WILD WULF IS INSIDE

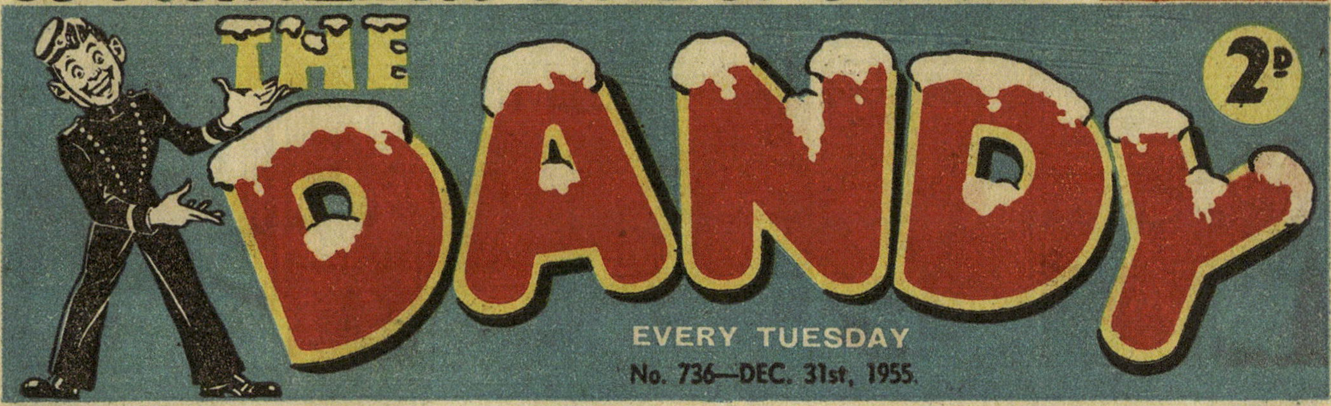


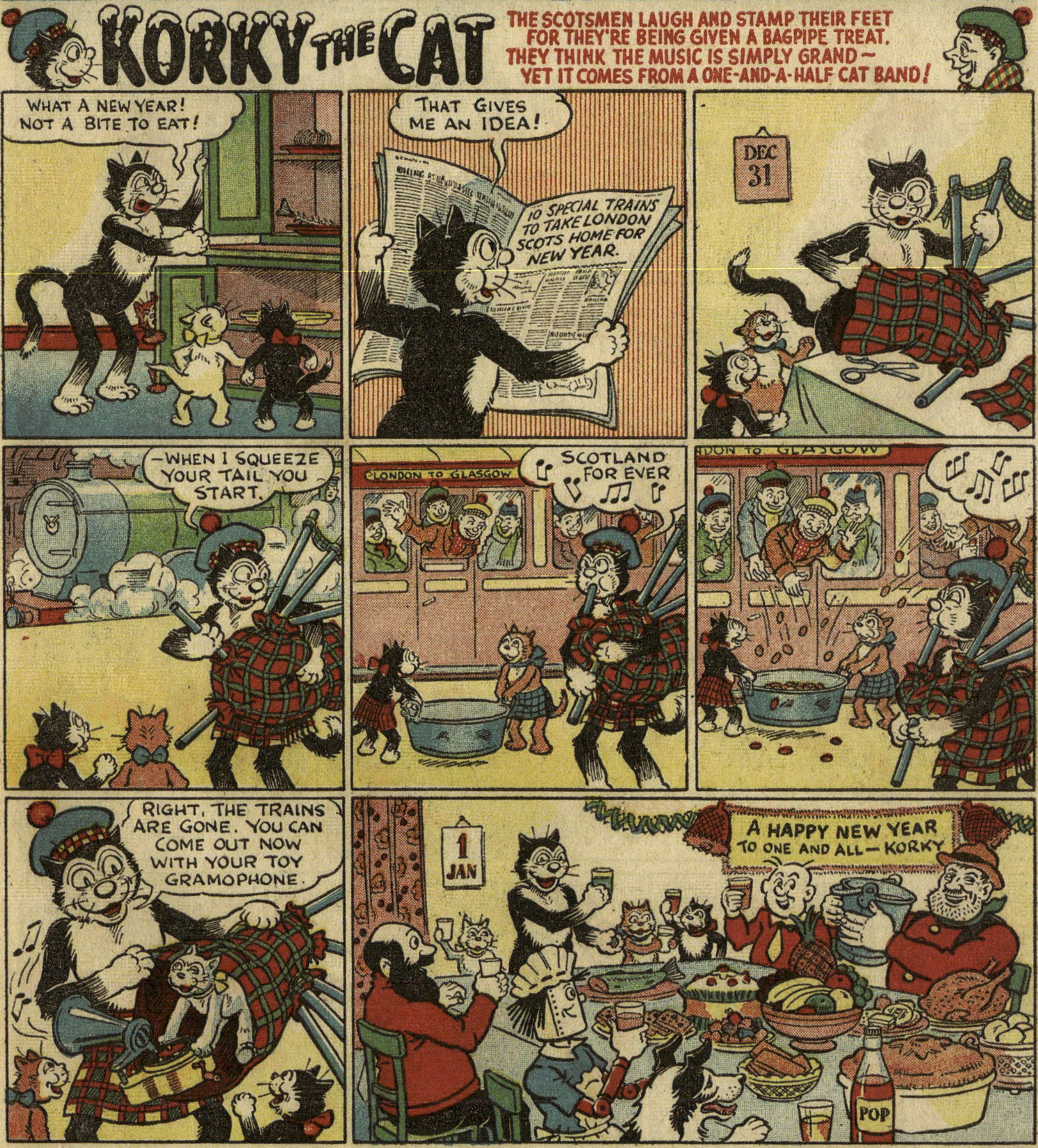

FIREWORKS FUN also
A GRAND NEW BLACK BOB STORY IN PICTURES
THE DANDY
2d
EVERY TUESDAY
No. 780—NOV 3rd, 1956.
KORKY THE CAT
FOLLOWING ONE OF HIS FIREWORKS TRICKS
KORKY LOOKS A RIGHT "GUY" ON A PILE OF BRICKS;
HE TRIED TO BE LIKE OLD GUY FAWKES
BUT FOUND HE'D BECOME JUST ONE OF THE CROCKS!
FIREWORKS
NOW FOR SOME GUY FAWKES FUN.
HI! GET AWAY FROM MY GRUB!
I'M GONNA FIX THESE MICE FOR GOOD.
THIS WILL FRIGHTEN THE LIVES OUT OF THEM.
HA-HA! THAT'S DONE THE TRICK!
RUN, LADS, RUN!
BANG!
HOME SWEET HOME
GEE, WHAT A BANG FOR A SIXPENNY BANGER!
YOU CRAZY CLOT— YOU RAN IT INTO A GAS-PIPE!

# KORKY THE CAT

Korky the Cat's looking quite a sight
Because he read from left to right.
He wouldn't have taken such an awful bashin'
If he'd read right to left in Chinese fashion!

HOLD YOUR EARS! HERE'S THE FIREWORKS FUN NUMBER

# THE DANDY

2d

EVERY TUESDAY

No. 885—NOV. 8th, 1958.

## KORKY THE CAT

Korky is King of Guy Fawkeses—
A Guy who has taken wings,
And all because he sat on a "throne"
Which was stuffed with bangers 'n' things!

Here's A HAPPY NEW YEAR—You'll Grin From Ear To Ear!
THE DANDY
2d
EVERY TUESDAY
No. 893—JAN. 3rd, 1959
KORKY THE CAT
Korky's New Year scheme at this gloomy house
Was as bright as a New Year pin;
For he turned a fence that kept folk out
Into one that brought them in!
NOBODY EVER COMES TO WISH ME A HAPPY NEW YEAR, KORKY.
IT'S THIS BIG FENCE YOU'VE GOT. IT KEEPS PEOPLE AWAY. LET ME CHANGE IT FOR YOU.
HAPPY NEW YEAR
SEE? CROWDS OF VISITORS NOW!
THE HAPPIEST NEW YEAR EVER—THANKS TO KORKY!

The DANDY, November 7, 1959.

# FIZZLING WITH FIREWORKS FUN!
# THE DANDY
**2ᴰ**

EVERY TUESDAY
No. 937—NOV. 7th, 1959.

## KORKY the CAT

The crows sit on a scarecrow,
But below them danger lurks —
It's all a plan of Korky's
To give them the fire-works!

1. "PENNY FOR THE GUY!"

2. "HUH! WE'VE COLLECTED NOTHING BUT BUTTONS AND FOREIGN COINS. THAT WON'T GET US A FIREWORKS DISPLAY."

3. "DRAT THESE CROWS! SHOO!"

4. "THEY'RE NOT SCARED OF MY SCARECROW." "THEY'LL BE SCARED OF OURS. GIVE ME TEN BOB AND I'LL SHOW YOU."

5. "OUR GUY MAKES A BETTER SCARECROW."

6. "YOU BET IT DOES! JUST WAIT FOR THIS!"

7. BANG! WHOOSH! BANG! "HA-HA! KORKY BOUGHT FIREWORKS WITH THAT TEN BOB!"

8. "GOOD FOR YOU, KORKY!"

The DANDY, November 5, 1960.

**FREE GIFTS For All Boys and Girls** SEE PAGE 3

# The Dandy

3d

EVERY TUESDAY    No. 989—NOV. 5th, 1960.

## KORKY the CAT

"I'M BROKE. ONE ROCKET AND ONE MATCH — THAT'S ALL I'VE GOT!"

"SAY, MISTER, CAN I COME AND SEE YOUR FIREWORKS SHOW?"

"PUSH OFF!"

"THE SELFISH ROTTER!"

"BUT I'LL SHOW HIM!"

CRASH!

SWISH  BANG  SWOOSH

"ONE ROCKET AND ONE MATCH — BUT WHAT A SHOW!"

# THE Dandy

3d

EVERY TUESDAY. No. 991—NOV. 19th, 1960.


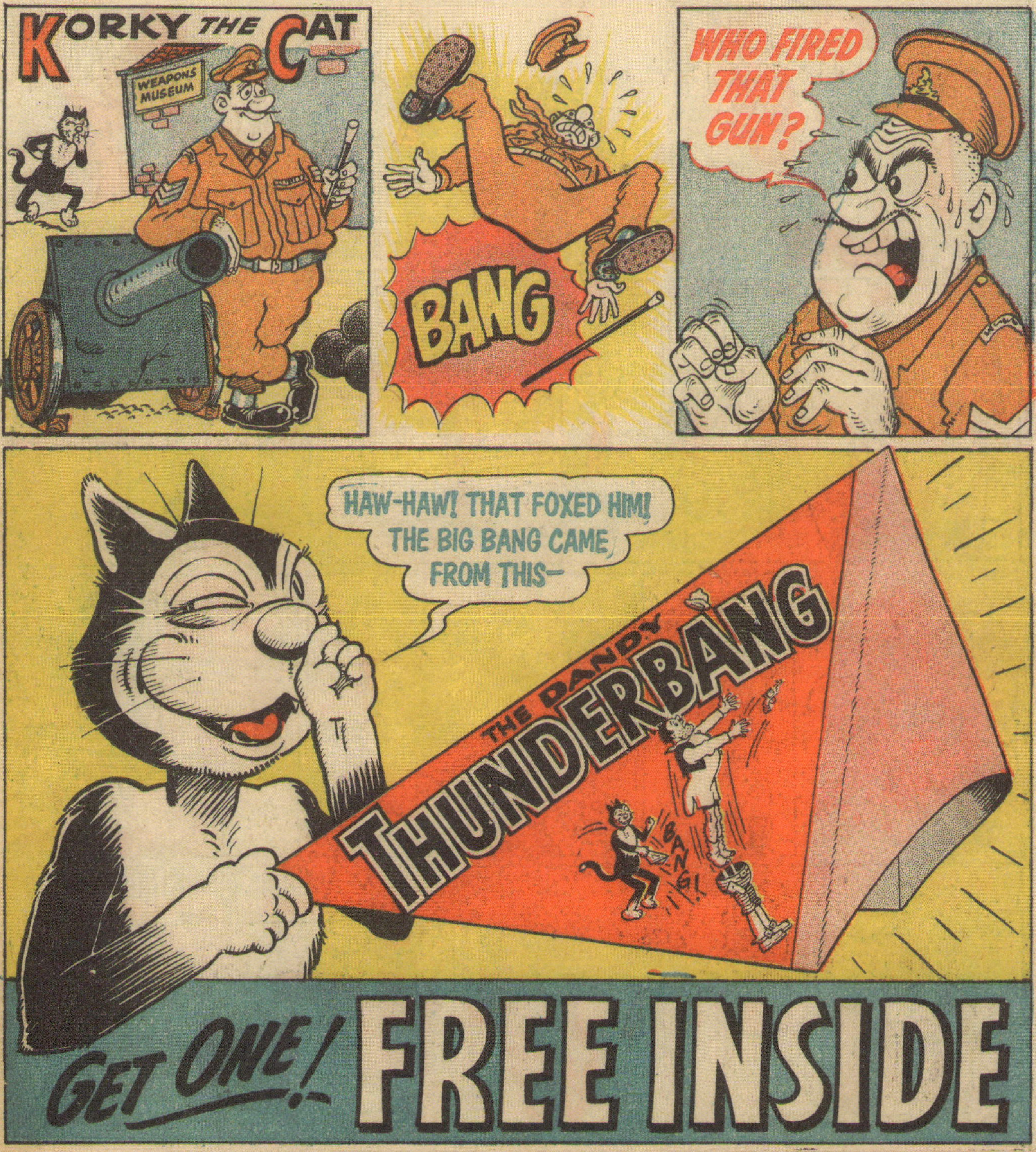

# THE Dandy

3d.

EVERY TUESDAY No. 997—DEC. 31st, 1960.

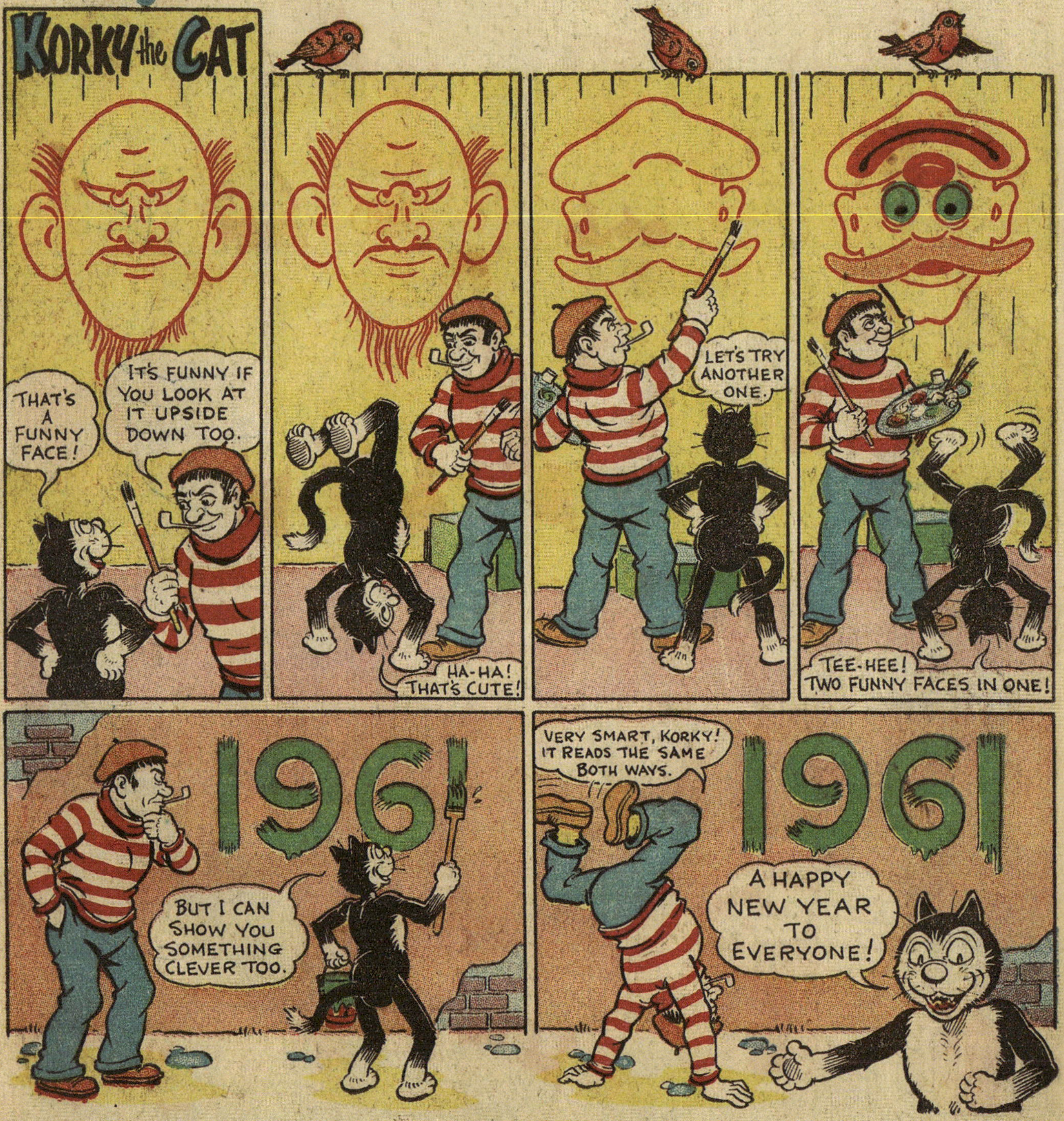

# The Dandy

**3d.**

EVERY TUESDAY
No. 1000—JAN. 21st, 1961.

## Korky the Cat

"This is my thousandth birthday, boys. I've appeared in 1000 issues of the 'Dandy.' I'm going off to get my present from the editor."

"We'll have to give Korky a present, too." "I've got an idea."

**WAREHOUSE** "Here are two in the woodpile."

**WAREHOUSE** "We got plenty in there."

"We'll pop his present through the letter box."

"Happy birthday, Korky. There's a thousand mice to keep you company."

# The Dandy

3D

EVERY TUESDAY   No. 1049—DECEMBER 30th, 1961.

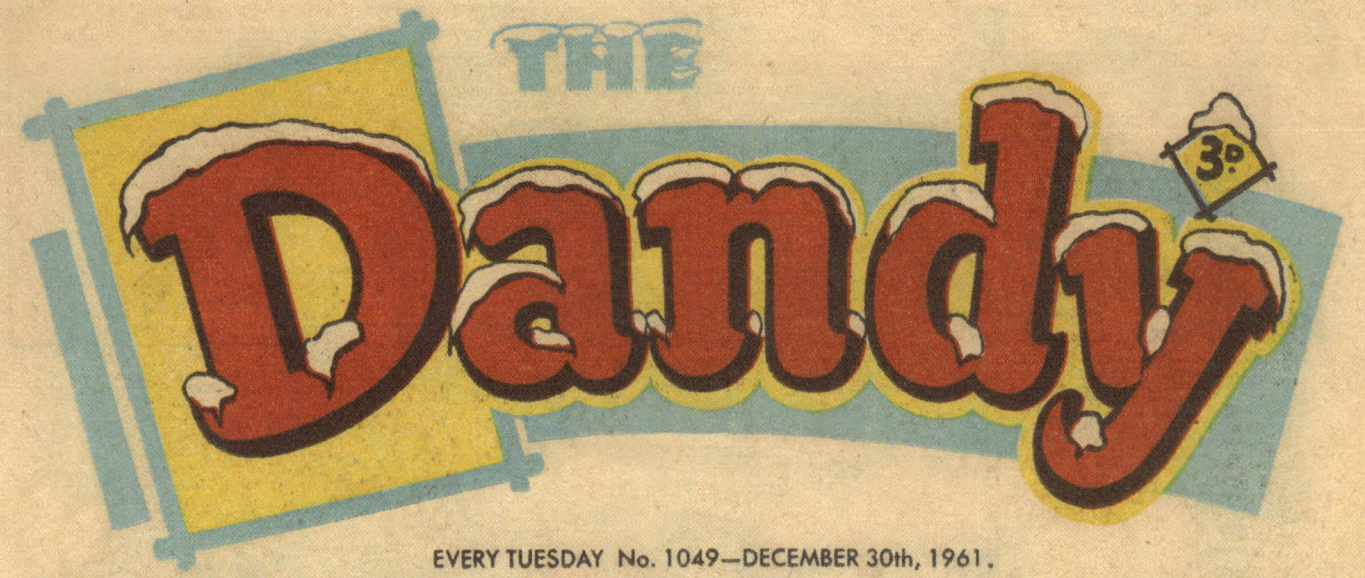

## Korky the Cat

**Panel 1:** Watch this!

**Panel 2:** Got 'im!

**Panel 3:** Just you wait!

**Panel 4:** Psst! He's right in front of that rickety old hoarding. One—two—three—

**Panel 5:** FIRE! ... G-G-Gosh!

**Panel 6:** A h-h-happy New Y-Year!

**Panel 7:** Yes—happy for us, Korky!

# THE Dandy

3D

EVERY TUESDAY. No. 1101—Dec. 29th, 1962.

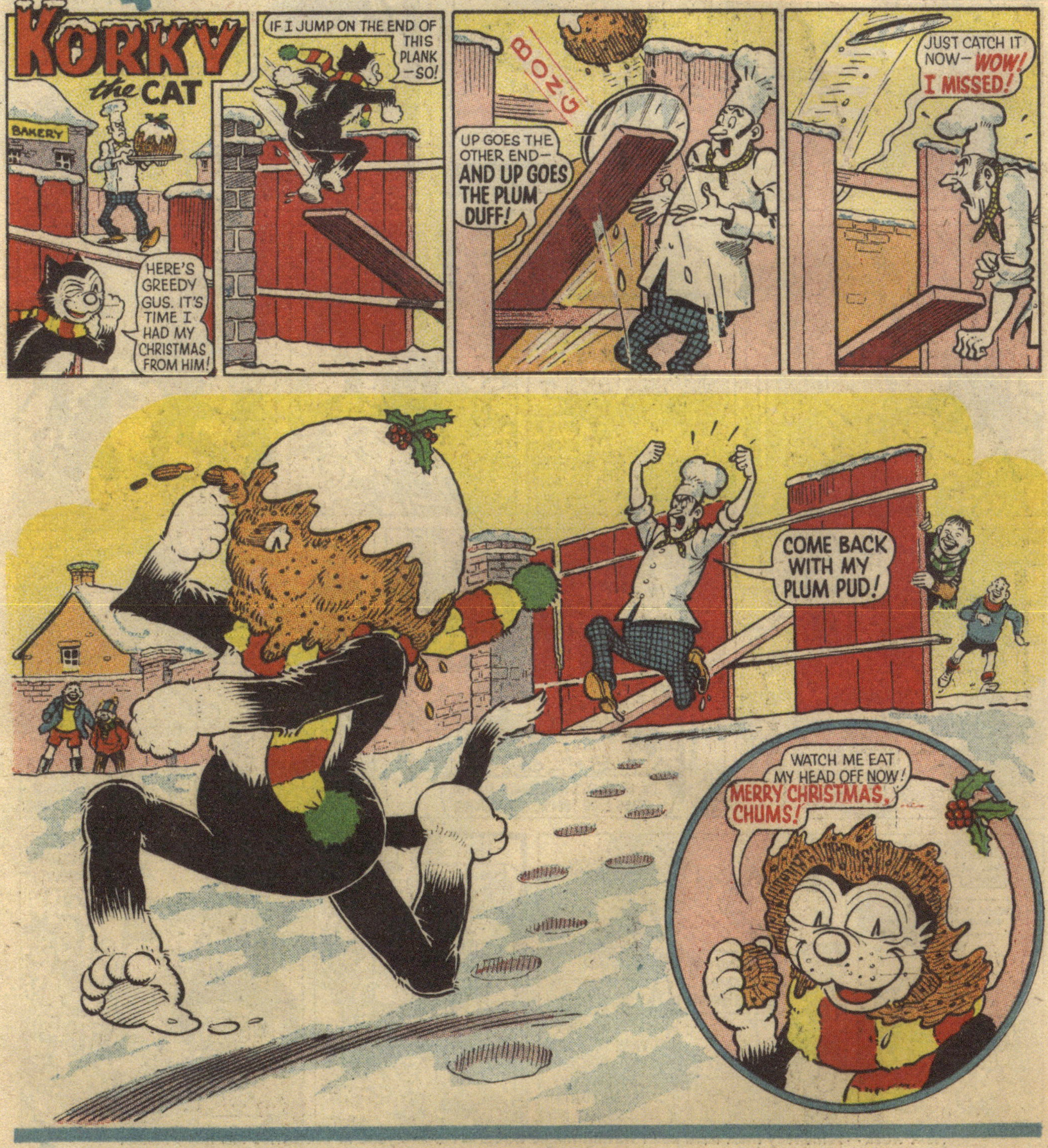

# The Dandy

3ᵈ

EVERY TUESDAY. No. 1102—Jan. 5th, 1963.

## KORKY THE CAT

"HAPPY NEW YEAR!"

SPLOSH!

SPLOSH!

# The Dandy

Every Tuesday. No. 1116—Apr. 13th, 1963.    3º

## Korky the Cat

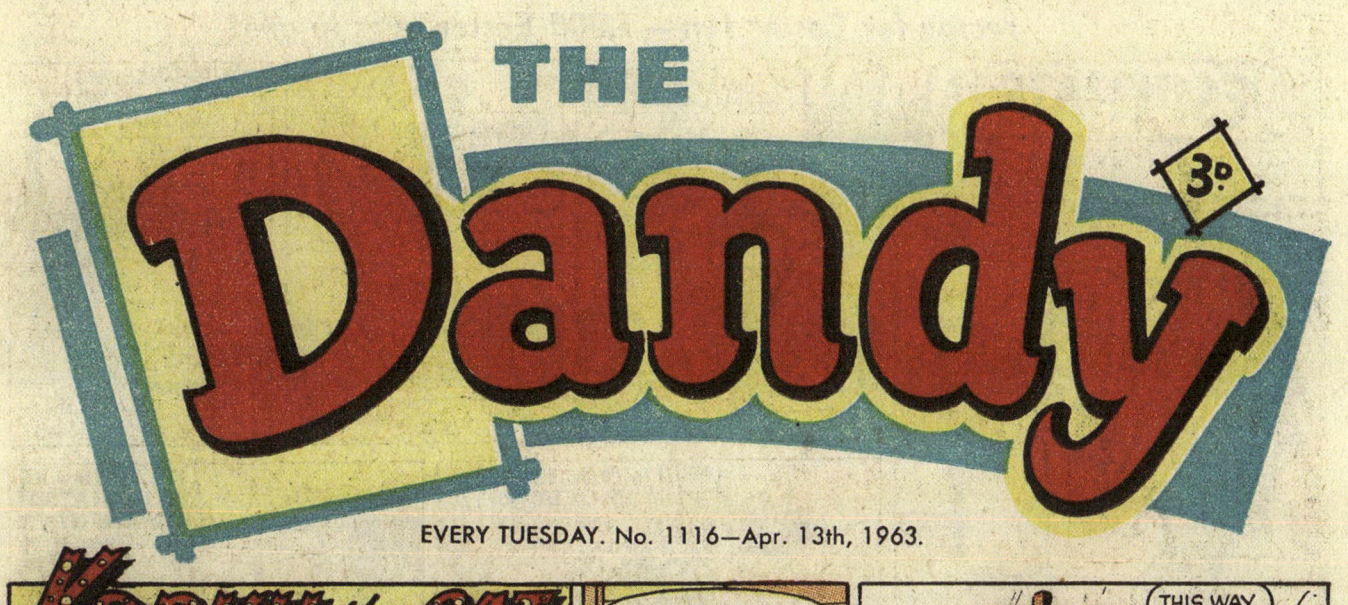

**Panel 1:** WE WERE GOING TO HAVE A PICNIC AND GO BOATING, UNCLE KORKY, BUT IT'S POURING RAIN. — DON'T WORRY, KITS — I'VE AN IDEA!

**Panel 2:** BUT WHAT ARE YOU DOING, UNCLE KORKY? — YOU'LL SOON SEE!

**Panel 3:** TO THE RIVER — THIS WAY, KITS!

**Panel 4:** HOW DO YOU LIKE OUR EASTER EGG GONDOLA? — HA! HA! WE'RE GOING BOATING AFTER ALL—AND HAVING A PICNIC!

# The Dandy

3ᵈ

EVERY TUESDAY. No. 1146—Nov. 9th, 1963.

## Korky THE CAT

**Panel 1:** NOW FOR SOME FIREWORKS FUN. FIRST A ROMAN CANDLE.

**Panel 2:** HEY, YOU ROTTER—YOU'VE PUT IT OUT!

**Panel 3:** KEEP YOUR HOSE TO YOURSELF WHILE I SET OFF A ROCKET.

**Panel 4:** BAH! HE'S DONE IT AGAIN!

**Panel 5:** HE'S GONE TO TEA. I'LL EMPTY MY FIREWORKS INTO HIS HOSE.

**Panel 6:** HAPPY FIREWORKS DAY, CHUMS! AND I BET MY CATHERINE WHEEL IS BIGGER THAN YOURS!

THE
Dandy
3D
EVERY TUESDAY. No. 1154—Jan. 4th, 1964.
KORKY the Cat
HI, MRS JONES!
HI, KORKY!
OH, GOSH! IT'S NEW YEAR TOMORROW—AND I HAVEN'T SENT MRS JONES A NEW YEAR CARD!
CLOSED
NEW YEAR Cards
TOO LATE! HOW CAN I SEND HER A NEW YEAR MESSAGE NOW?
AH! I KNOW!
GOOD—THE FROST'S JUST BEGINNING TO STIFFEN THE CLOTHES UP.
NEXT MORNING.
From KORKY
OH, THANK YOU, KORKY!
AND THE SAME GOES FOR EVERYBODY!

# The Dandy

EVERY TUESDAY. No. 1158—Feb. 1st, 1964.

3º

## Korky the Cat

**Panel 1:** OOH! WHAT A DIN!

**Panel 2:** THAT NIGHT, WHEN KORKY IS ASLEEP. ZZZZZ

**Panel 3:** AND NEXT MORNING. HEY! LOOK AT MY GUITAR!

**Panel 4:** THAT NIGHT. BAH! I CAN'T SLEEP! THEY'RE PRACTISING ON THE GUITARS THEY MADE OUT OF MINE.

**Panel 5:** LATER NEXT DAY. HEY! WHAT'S GOING ON IN MY HOUSE?

**Panel 6:** (Korky shocked at window)

**Panel 7:** The fabulous BEATLE MICE — SHE LOVES CHEESE! YEAH! YEAH! YEAH! — WE LOVE THE BEATLEMICE! — SCREAM

# Dandy

3d

EVERY TUESDAY. No. 1166—Mar. 28th, 1964.

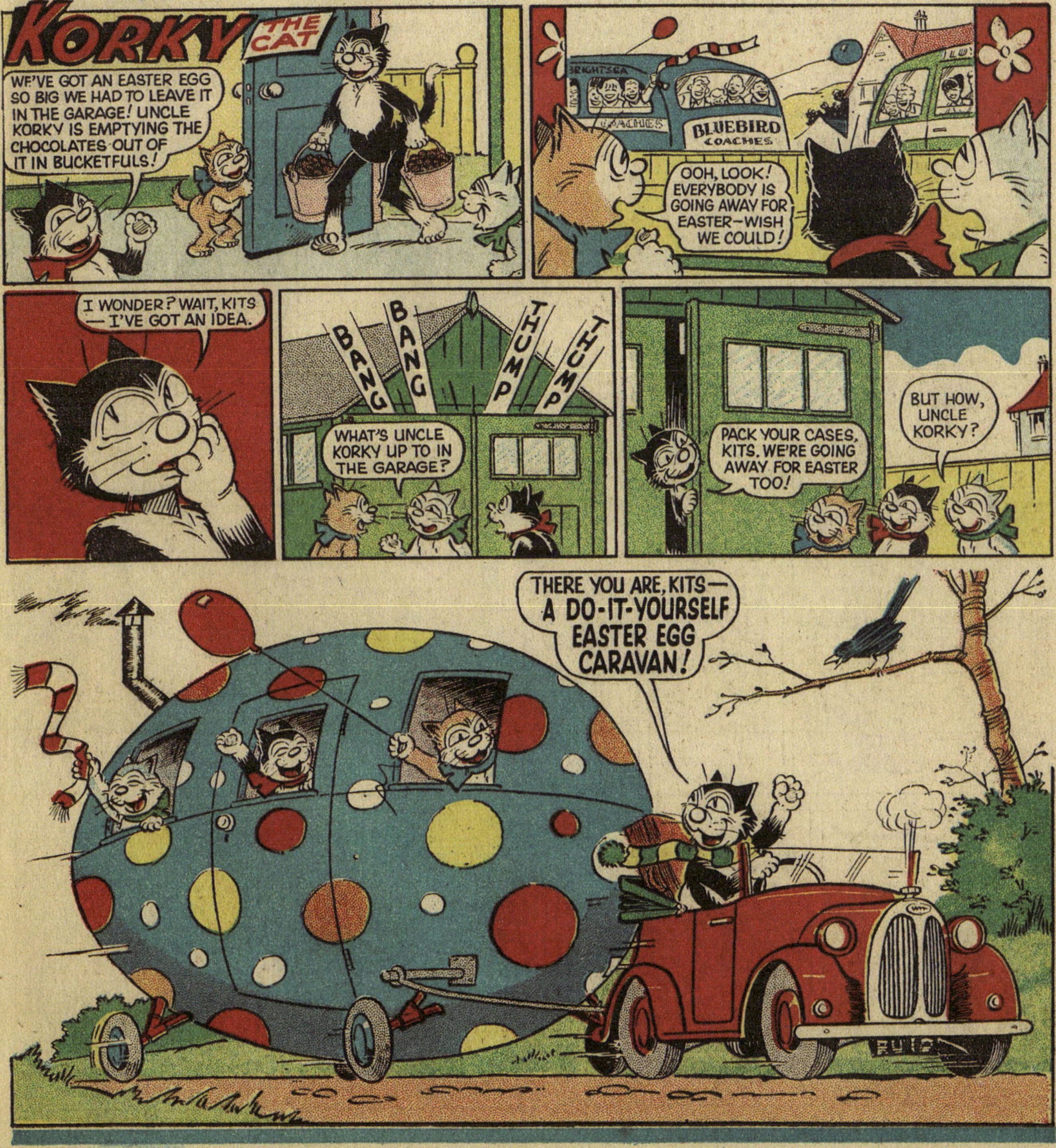

# THE Dandy

3d

EVERY TUESDAY. No. 1198—Nov. 7th, 1964.


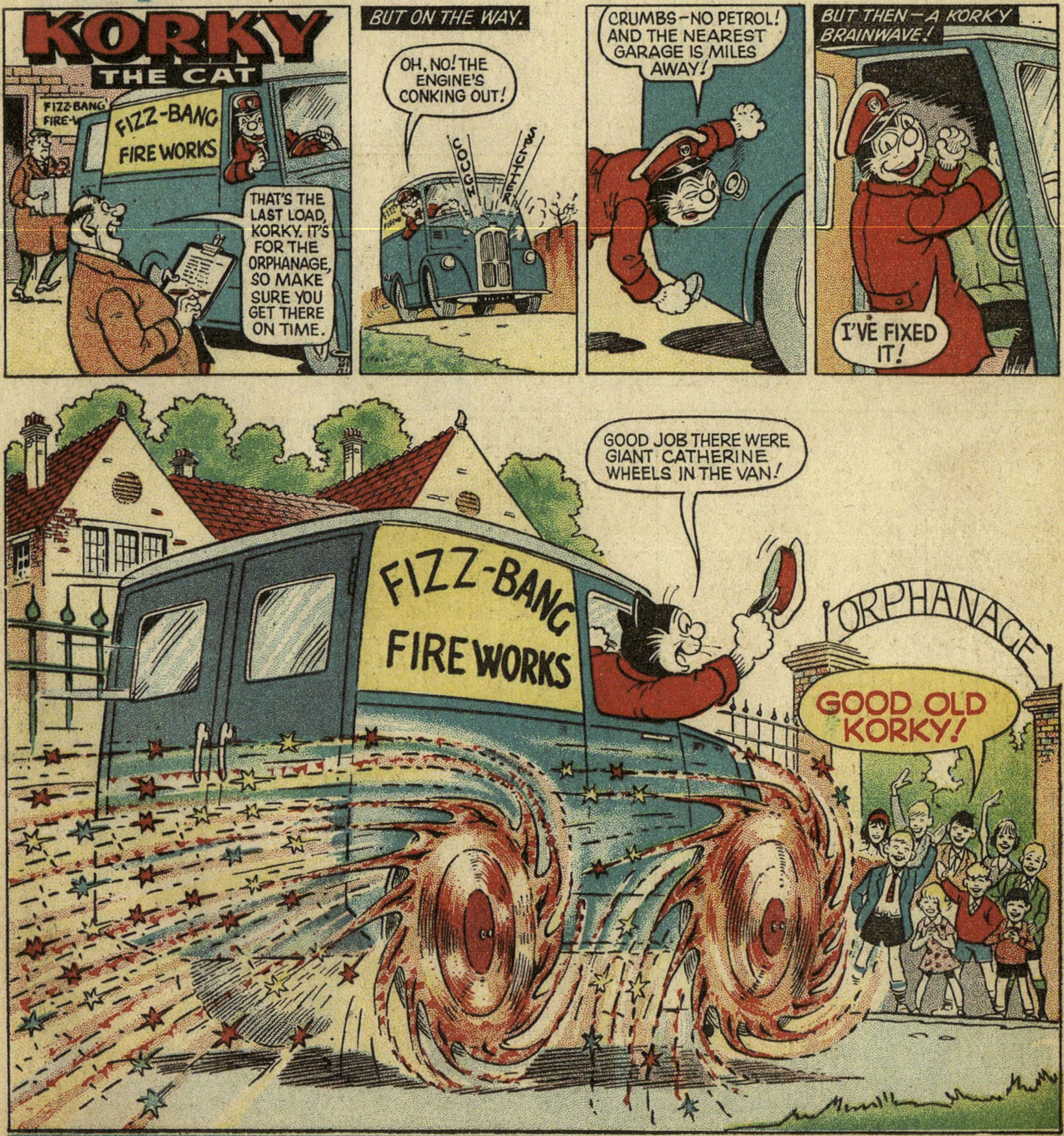

# THE Dandy

3D.

EVERY TUESDAY. No. 1219—APR. 3rd, 1965.


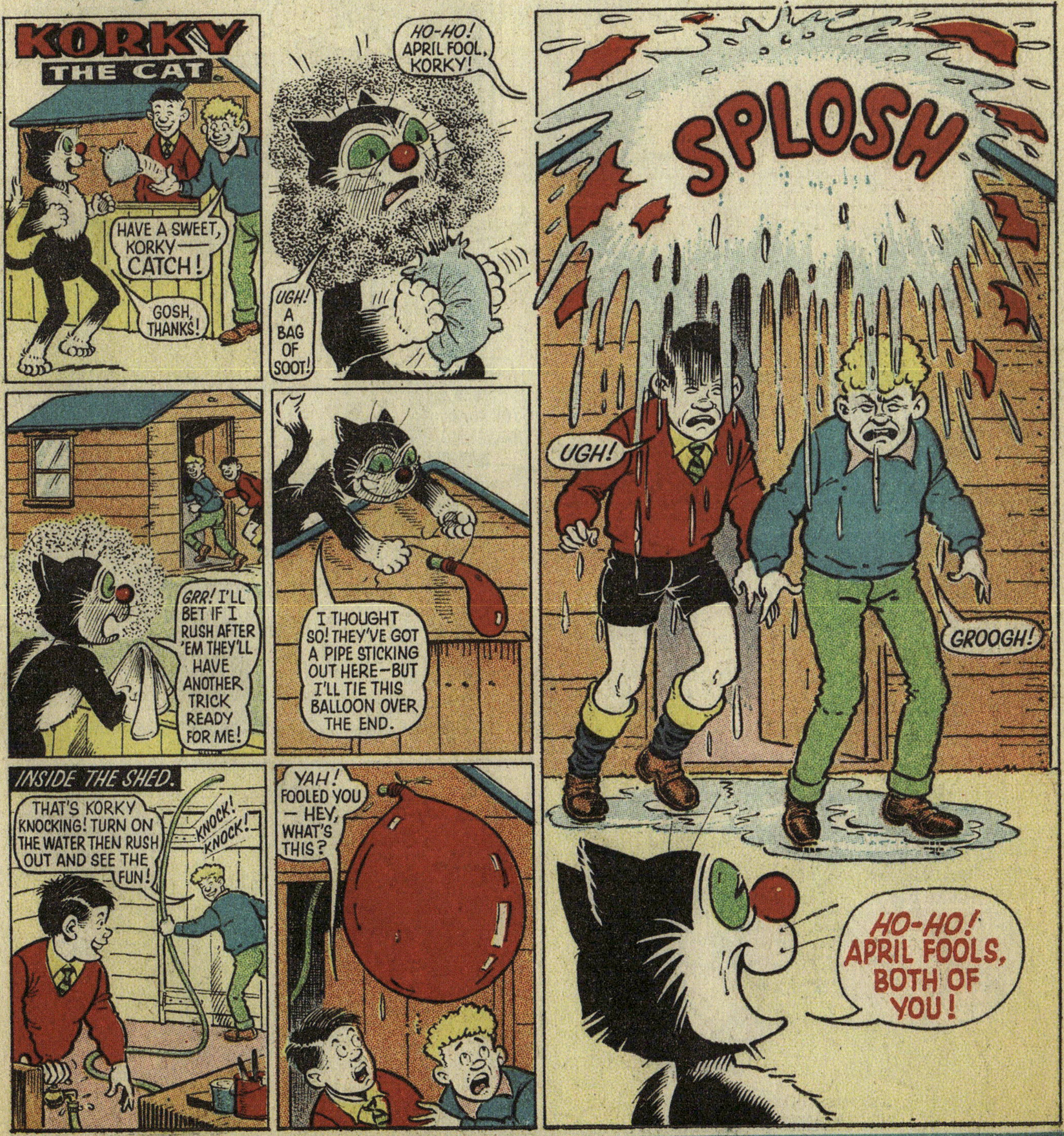

# The Dandy

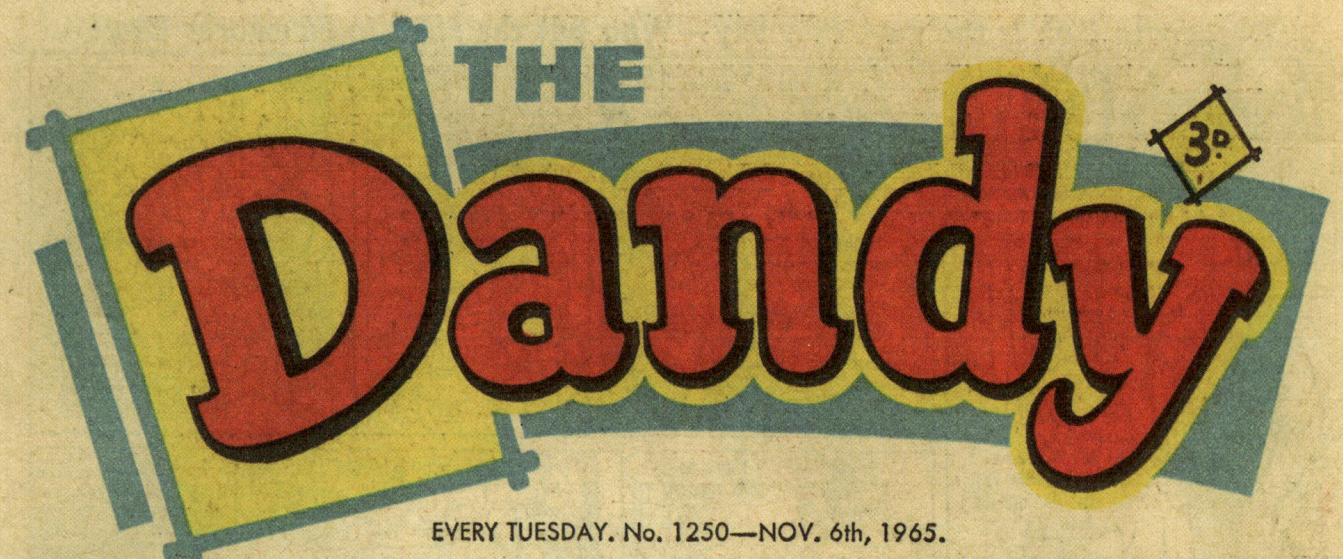

Every Tuesday. No. 1250—NOV. 6th, 1965. 3°

## Korky THE CAT

**Panel 1:** Hey, Percy! I've found a snooper on our island!

**Panel 2:** We'll row you over to the mainland. We're not sharing our fireworks with you or anybody!

**Panel 3:** HEH-HEH! I've pulled out the bung—but I'll keep my foot on the hole till I'm ashore!

**Panel 4:** Take that—and scram!

**Panel 5:** *But when they start to row back—* Oh, no! The boat's leaking! There's why! That's your bung!

**Panel 6:** And now I know how to get to the island!

**Panel 7:** A dustbin lid fitted with rockets!

# The Dandy

3D

Every Tuesday. No. 1304—NOV. 19th, 1966.

## Korky the Cat

**Panel 1:** THIS IS WHERE I'M GOING TO HANG MY NEW MIRROR.

**Panel 2:** GOLLY! THERE'S A WATER PIPE BEHIND THAT BOARD. SPLOSH

**Panel 3:** I'LL PLUG THE HOLE WITH A PIECE OF CHEWING GUM.

**Panel 4:** THAT'S FIXED IT UNTIL I CAN GET A PLUMBER.

**Panel 5:** OH, NO! IT'S BUBBLE GUM!

**Panel 6:** BATHROOM — CRASH! SPLOSH

# The Dandy

**3ᵈ**

EVERY TUESDAY. No. 1310—DEC. 31st., 1966.

## KORKY THE CAT

**Korky:** Watch this, folks—I've got a smashing idea!

**But when the bobbies move off—**
**Korky:** Dash it! The trick hasn't worked because they've changed places... I'll have to change them back again!

**And so—**
**Korky:** Help! Police! There's a desperate criminal in here! Bring your handcuffs!

**Korky:** What's happening?
**Bobby:** Where is he?
**Bobby:** I can't see a thing!
CLICK CLICK
**Korky:** Got 'em! Now to let 'em out!

**Korky:** They couldn't see in the dark—but I could!

**HAPPY NEW YEAR**

**Korky:** Now you see why I had to handcuff them together!

# The Dandy

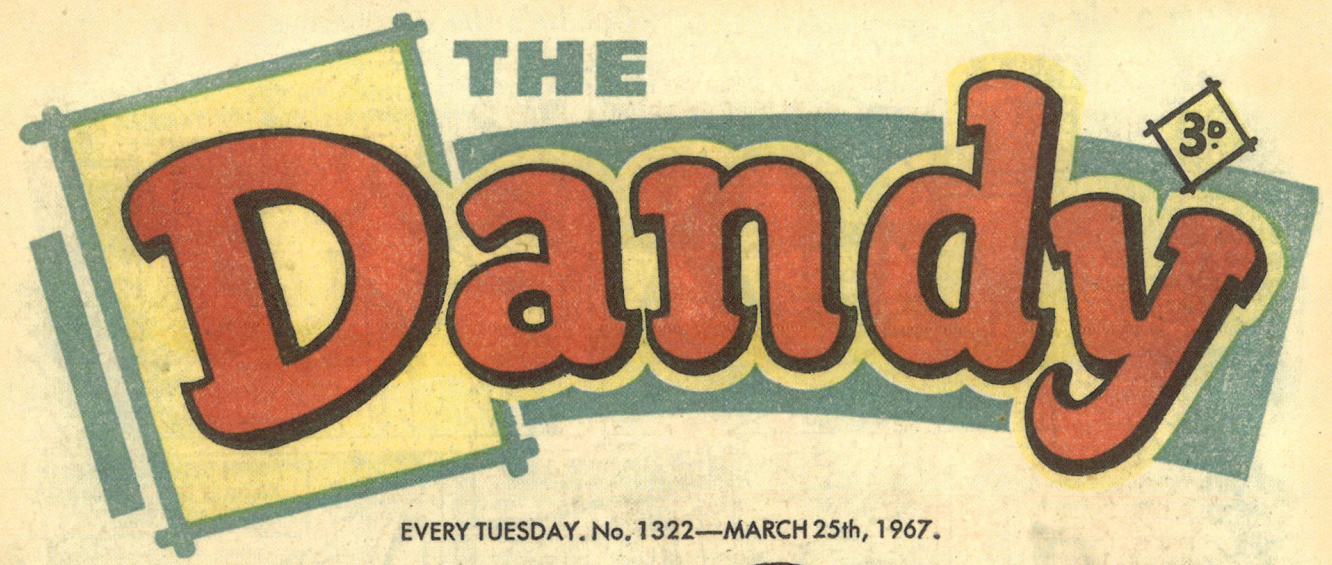

Every TUESDAY. No. 1322—MARCH 25th, 1967.

## Korky the Cat

**Panel 1:** IT'S FROM YOUR FRIENDS THE MICE, KORKY!

**Panel 2:** MY FRIENDS? HUH! I WONDER WHAT'S IN IT?

**Panel 3:** COULD BE A BOXING GLOVE. *THUMP*

**Panel 4:** OR A TIME BOMB! *BOOM*

**Panel 5:** WE'LL SOON FIND OUT! *SNIP* — HORRIBLE PONG

**Panel 6:** HO-HO! IT'S AN EASTER EGG MADE OF CHEESE!—AND IT WAS MEANT FOR US—NOT YOU, KORKY! PONG — GROOGH

# THE Dandy

3d

EVERY TUESDAY. No. 1359—DEC. 9th, 1967.


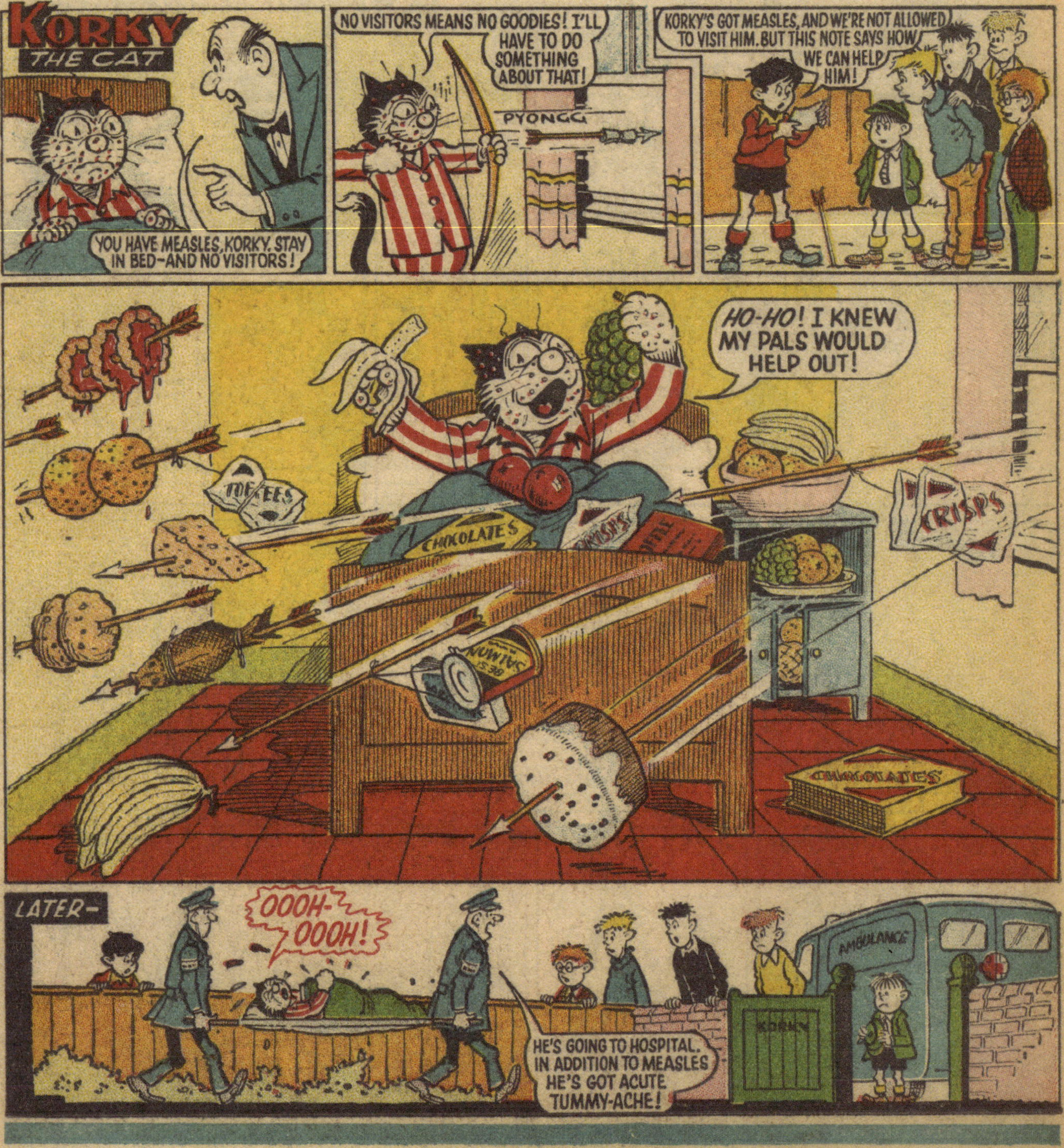

# THE Dandy

4d

EVERY TUESDAY. No. 1398—SEPT. 7th, 1968.


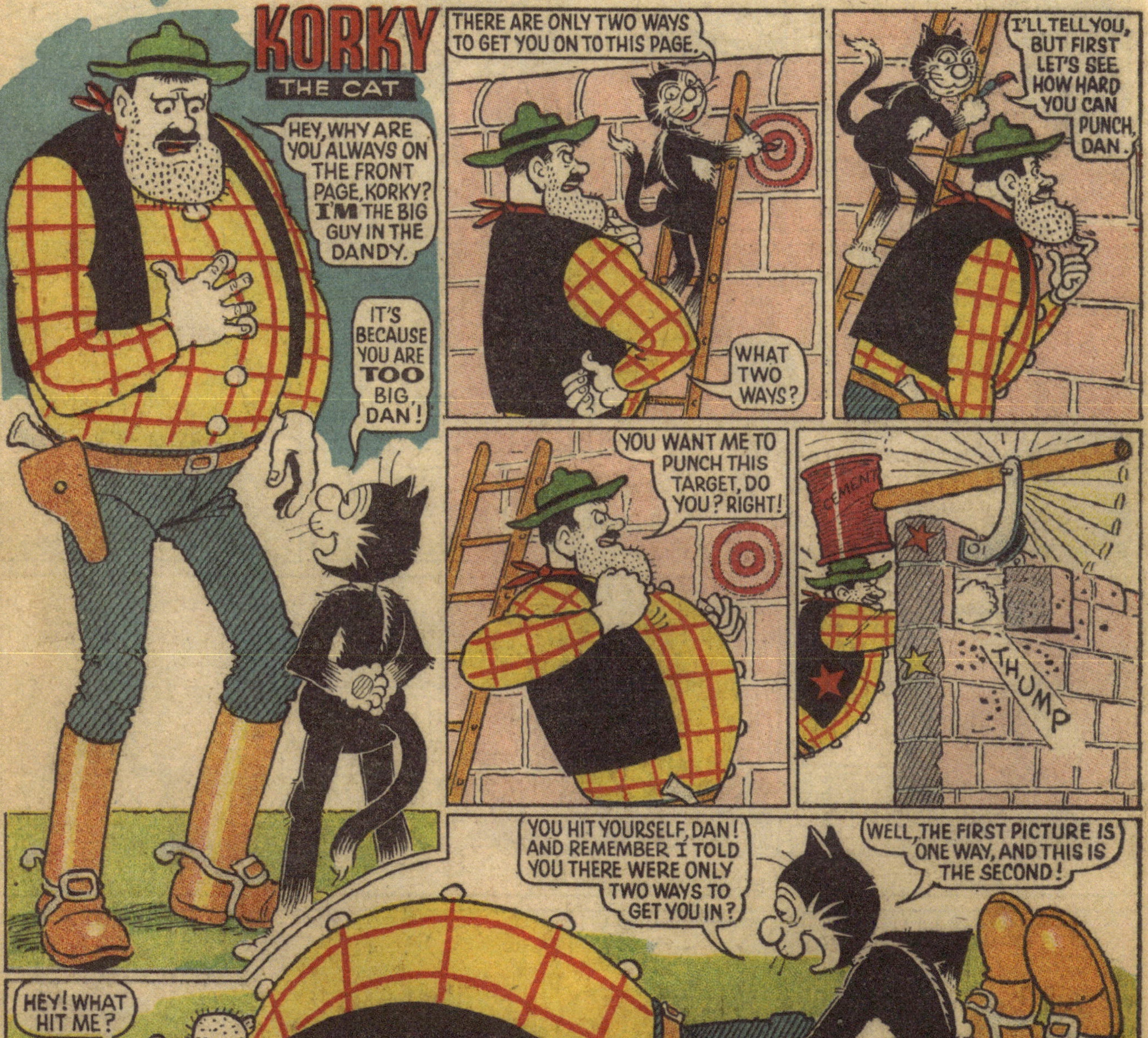

# The Dandy

4ᴰ

Every Tuesday. No. 1415—JAN. 4th, 1969.

## KORKY THE CAT

**SHIVER STAMP:** BRR! NO COAL FOR MY FIRE AND IT'S FREEZING.

NEVER MIND! THIS IS THE THING TO KEEP ME WARM!

CRASH

AH, WELL, MY SLEDGE IS STILL KEEPING ME WARM! HAPPY NEW YEAR!

JAN 1

# THE Dandy 4d

EVERY TUESDAY. No. 1518—DEC. 26th, 1970

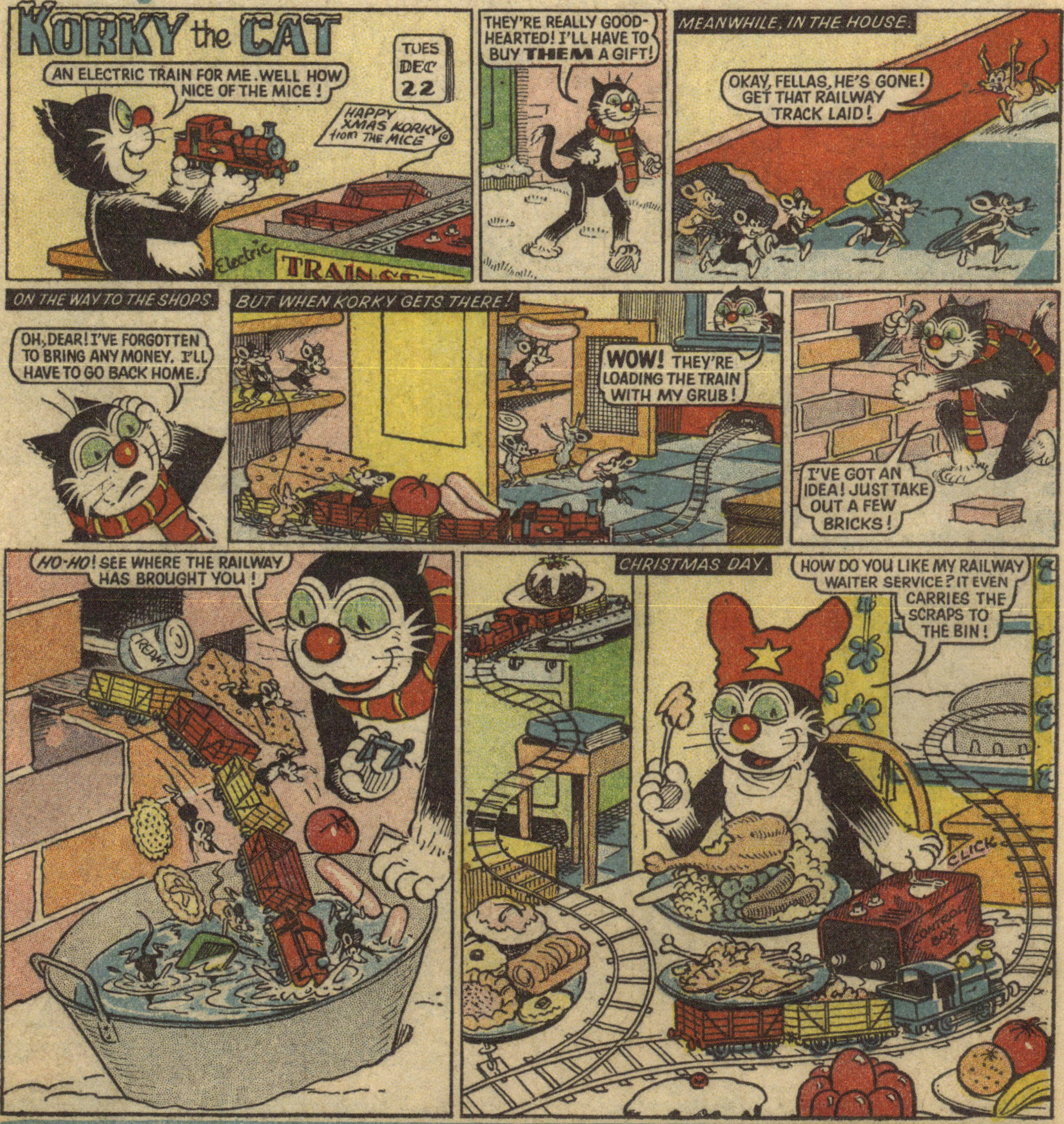

# THE Dandy

**2p**

Every Tuesday. NO. 1526—FEB. 20th, 1971.

## KORKY the CAT

**Panel 1:** WONDER WHAT THAT MEANS? — THIS IS "D" DAY!

**Panel 2:** THEN— ALL KINDS OF PETS FOR SALE. PET SHOP. PERHAPS IT MEANS "D" FOR DOGGIE DAY!

**Panel 3:** YEOWP! GRRR! ALL KINDS OF PETS FOR SALE.

**Panel 4:** THE BIG BULLY! I WASN'T GOING TO HARM HER PUPS!

**Panel 5:** HEY! IT COULD BE "D" FOR DUSTBIN DAY. BAKERY!

**Panel 6:** HERE YOU ARE, FELLOWS! HAVE SOME DOUGHNUTS! GOSH! IT MIGHT BE "D" FOR DOUGHNUT DAY! BAKERY. DELICIOUS DOUGH—

**Panel 7:** BUT IT ISN'T ANY OF THESE THINGS! HO-HO! NOW I KNOW! IT'S "D" FOR "DANDY" DAY! NEWSAGENT. THE DANDY IS ON SALE HERE.

AND, OF COURSE, IT'S ALSO "D" FOR DECIMAL DAY! YOU'D BETTER HAVE YOUR NEW PENNIES READY, KORKY!

# The New Big Dandy

EVERY TUESDAY.

**2p**

NO. 1530
MARCH 20th, 1971.

## Korky the Cat

"HEE-HEE! WHAT A LAUGH!"

"HERE COMES DESPERATE DAN. WATCH ME PLAY A TRICK ON HIM!"

RAT-TAT-TAT

"WHO'S FIRING A MACHINE GUN?"

"HA-HA! IT ISN'T A MACHINE GUN, DAN!"

"IT'S THIS RED RACKETTY!"

THE RED RACKETTY

FIX HEAVY BUTTON OR COIN HERE

RAT-TAT-TAT-TAT-TAT-

**GET ONE FREE INSIDE!**

The Dandy
A MERRY CHRISTMAS NUMBER
2p
EVERY TUESDAY.
No. 1675
DEC. 29th, 1973

# The Dandy

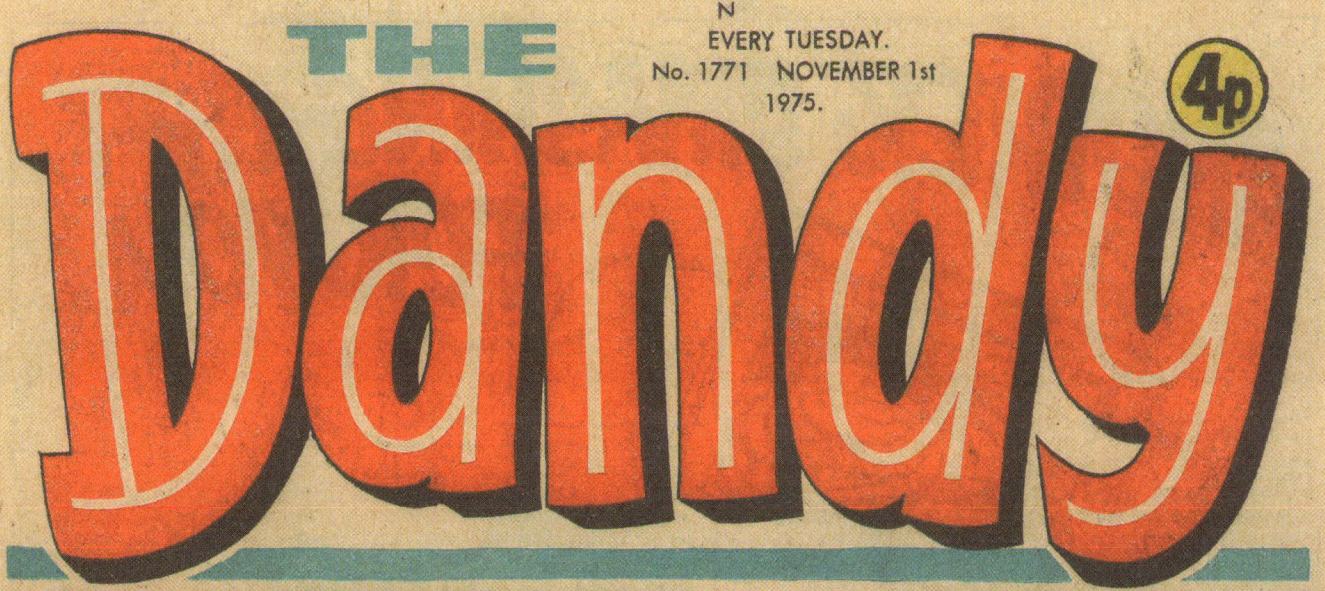

N Every Tuesday.
No. 1771  NOVEMBER 1st 1975.
4p

## Korky the Cat

HA-HA-HA!
HO-HO!
HEE-HEE!
HA-HA-HA!

WHAT'S GOING ON?

I MUST FIND OUT.

HA-HA-HA!
HO-HO-HO!
HEE-HEE!
HO-HO-HO!

WHY, IT'S SOMEBODY WEARING MY FACE!

IT'S A MASK, KORKY — AND SEE HOW IT GLOWS IN THE DARK!

**THE KORKY GLOW-MASK** — GET IT! **FREE** INSIDE!

# The Dandy

**No. 1832**
**JAN. 1st, 1977**
4p
EVERY TUESDAY

## KORKY the CAT

OH, BOY! LOOK! MY NEW NEIGHBOUR MUST BE HAVING A NEW YEAR PARTY!

YOUR ORDER, SIR.

RIGHT! BRING IT ALL IN!

AND YOU CAN BUZZ OFF! YOU'RE NOT INVITED, SEE!

*SLAP!*

WE'LL SEE ABOUT THAT! I'VE GOT A SCHEME!

LATER—

I'VE MADE A BIG HAPPY NEW YEAR SIGN. IS IT O.K. IF I JOIN IT TO YOUR HOUSE?

I SUPPOSE SO. BUT YOU'RE STILL NOT INVITED TO MY PARTY!

THANKS! I'LL JUST TIE IT TO THIS NAIL!

YOU MUST BE MAD WASTING YOUR TIME ON A THING LIKE THAT!

WE'LL SOON SEE IF I WAS WASTING MY TIME.

**HAPPY NEW YEAR**

HEE-HEE! HE'S GONE OUT AND LEFT THE WINDOW OPEN!

ZZZ ZZZ

OPEN THIS DOOR! THUMP! BANG! DO YOU HEAR?

# THE Dandy

5p

No. 1919
September 2nd,
1978.

EVERY TUESDAY


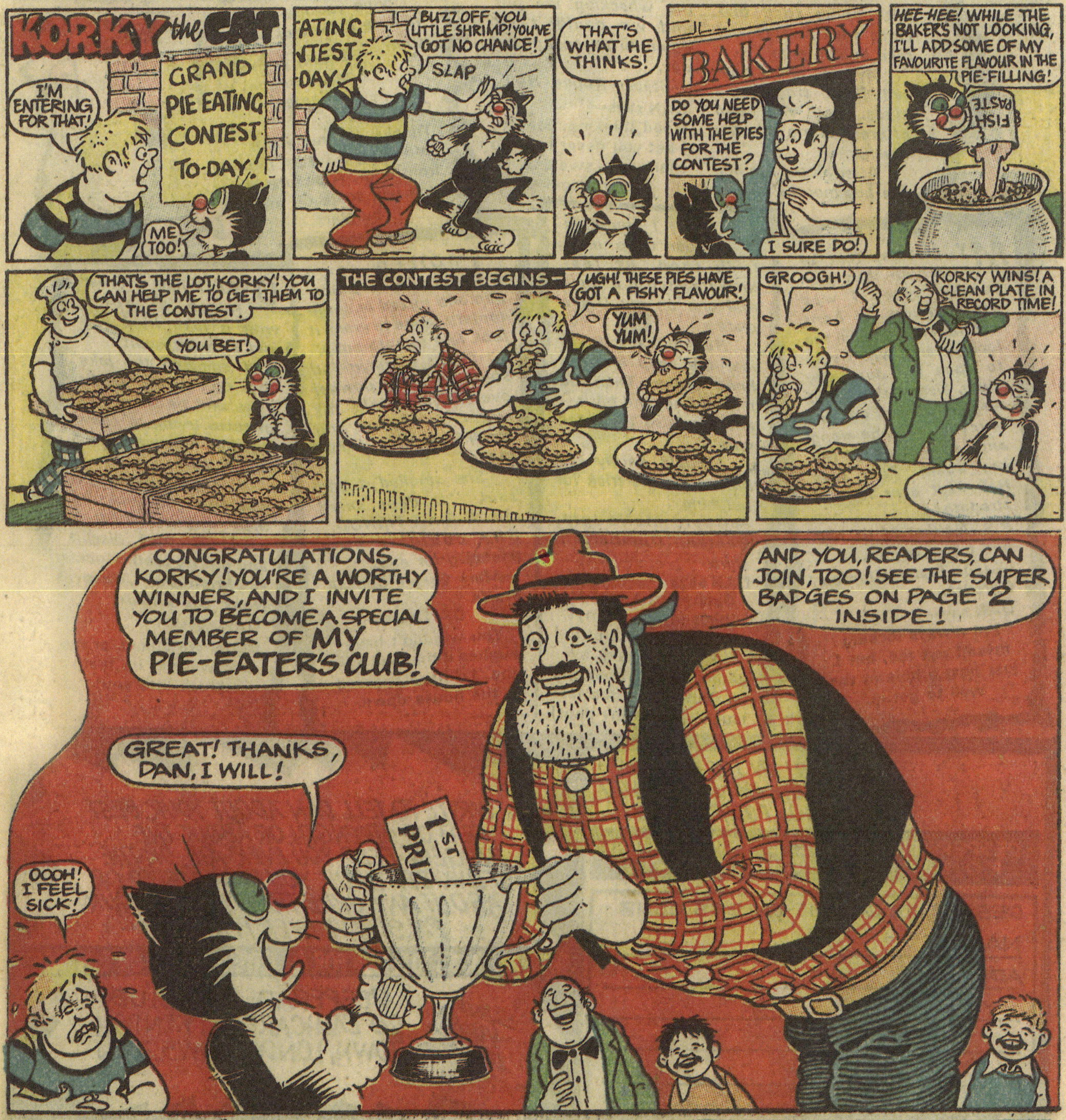

# The Dandy

**BUMPER XMAS NUMBER**

6p

EVERY TUESDAY

No. 1936
December 30th, 1978.

## KORKY the CAT

**Panel 1:** THERE'S TWENTY PENCE, KORKY, FOR CHOPPING UP MY FIREWOOD! — THANKS, MR. HILL!

**Panel 2:** MR HILL'S DOG ARRIVES — AARGH! — I HATE CATS!

**Panel 3:** OH, NO! MY MONEY AND MY HOUSE-KEY HAVE LANDED IN THAT PLUM DUFF MIXTURE!

**Panel 4:** WELL, I'M NOT GETTING THEM OUT — AND I'M NOT PAYING YOU AGAIN! SO BUZZ OFF WHILE I COOK MY PLUM DUFF!

**Panel 5:** LATER — AH! THE PLUM DUFF IS MADE, AND THAT CHOP ON THE TABLE GIVES ME AN IDEA!

**Panel 6:** I'LL HANG IT ON HIS BACK AND WAIT FOR ROVER TO SNIFF IT!

**Panel 7:** I HAD A CHOP ON THAT PLATE — WHERE HAS IT GONE?

**Panel 8:** THEN — HEY! THERE'S THE CHOP — OH, NO! LET GO, ROVER! — SNATCH

**Panel 9:** BRING IT BACK AT ONCE, ROVER! — HA-HA! THAT WILL KEEP HIM BUSY!

**Panel 10:** BACK HOME — I CAN'T GET INTO THE HOUSE UNTIL I'VE FOUND MY DOOR-KEY. BUT IT'S IN THE PLUM-DUFF SOMEWHERE, AND I'M HAVING A SUPER TIME SEARCHING FOR IT! YUM-YUM! — HAPPY CHRISTMAS, EVERYONE!

# The Dandy

**CLUB BADGES TO BE HAD FROM DESPERATE DAN! See Inside**

6p

No. 1937
January 6th, 1979.

EVERY TUESDAY

## KORKY the CAT

"Any knives for me to grind?"

*KNIVES SCISSORS GROUND*

"Poor man! I'll give him something to do."

"Will you sharpen these scissors for me?"

"Certainly!"

"I'll have them done in a jiffy, Korky."

"Now let me test them out for you, Korky."

"Okay!"

"Gosh! A fancy paper design! That's clever! You must come to my New Year party."

AT THE PARTY—
"I've folded the paper up in a special way. Now, watch this."

"And when the paper is unfolded, look what it says!"

# A HAPPY NEW YEAR

# THE Dandy

**DESPERATE DAN WANTS YOU TO JOIN HIS CLUB!** See Page 2

**6p**

No. 1951 — April 14th, 1979

EVERY TUESDAY

## KORKY the CAT

**OH, BOY! I MUST TRY FOR THAT PRIZE!**

*EASTER FESTIVAL — PRIZE for the EGG with the FUNNIEST FACE!*

**THIS IS A GOOD FUNNY FACE! HEE-HEE! LET'S SMASH KORKY'S EASTER EGG!**

**OO! WHAT A SHAME! IT'S BROKEN!** — PUSH — CRASH

**LATER ON — LOOK! HE'S PAINTING ANOTHER ONE.**

**WE'LL SMASH THIS ONE, TOO!**

**IT DIDN'T BREAK! — OF COURSE NOT! IT'S MADE OF RUBBER!** BOUNCE BOUNCE

**AND BECAUSE IT'S MADE OF RUBBER, IT CAN SQUEEZE UP INTO LOTS OF FUNNY FACES! HAPPY EASTER!**

*EASTER EGG FUNNY FACE COMPETITION*

**KORKY WINS!**

# The Dandy

**GREAT NEW PAGES of FUN Inside**

7p

No. 1976 OCT 6th, 1979

EVERY TUESDAY

## KORKY the CAT

**FIZZ** **CRACKLE**
WHAT'S UP WITH DESPERATE DAN?

SOUNDS AS THOUGH HE'S SWALLOWED A BOX OF BULLETS!

CAREFUL, DAN! DON'T EXPLODE!

I WON'T! I'M EATING POP ROCKS — AND THEY'RE LOTS TASTIER THAN BULLETS! TRY THEM, KORKY!

FIZZ CRACKLE

THEY'RE MAGIC!

**GET YOUR POP ROCKS FREE INSIDE!**

# THE Dandy

To All Readers MERRY CHRISTMAS!

TREAT YOURSELF BY JOINING THE CLUB ON PAGE 2

7p

No. 1988
Dec 29th,
1979.

EVERY TUESDAY

# The Dandy

**No 2000! SPECIAL CELEBRATION ISSUE!**

7p

EVERY TUESDAY

No. 2000 March 22nd, 1980.

## Korky the Cat

"WHAT'S THAT YOU'VE GOT THERE, KORKY?"
"THIS IS THE BIRTHDAY CAKE FOR THE DANDY'S 2000TH ISSUE! I'M GOING TO HAVE A PARTY!"

"THE GAMEY DIDN'T KNOW THESE ARE SPECIAL CANDLES. I JUST FIT THEM TOGETHER, SO—"

"AND THEY MAKE A SMASHING FISHING ROD!"

NO FISHING

**LATER—** "HEY! HAVE YOU BEEN FISHING?"
"FISHING? HOW COULD I WITHOUT A ROD?"

TO THE RIVER

"HEE-HEE! THE GAMEY WOULD HAVE A FIT IF HE KNEW THE SECRET OF THIS CAKE!"

"IT'S HOLLOW—AND LOOK WHAT I HID INSIDE IT!"

"HAPPY BIRTHDAY TO ME— AND TO THE DANDY!"

# The Dandy

**BE A PIE-EATER!** AND WEAR A **DESPERATE DAN** BADGE! See Page 2

8p

No. 2041
January 3rd, 1981.

EVERY TUESDAY

## Korky the Cat

**Korky:** I'M GOING TO A NEW YEAR PARTY TONIGHT!

**Officer:** PULL OVER, KORKY!
**Korky:** WHAT'S WRONG, OFFICER?

**Officer:** YOU HAVEN'T GOT A RED REFLECTOR. THAT'S AGAINST THE LAW, YOU KNOW!
**Korky:** SORRY, OFFICER.

**Korky:** I'LL BE ABLE TO PICK UP A REFLECTOR FROM ONE OF THESE SCRAP BIKES.

**Korky:** SAY, THIS REFLECTOR GIVES ME A GREAT IDEA!

**Korky:** THAT'S THE FIRST ONE!

**Officer:** WHAT ARE YOU UP TO NOW, KORKY?
**Korky:** SHINE YOUR HEADLIGHTS ON THIS WALL AND YOU'LL SEE!

*HAPPY NEW YEAR*

**Officer:** AND A HAPPY NEW YEAR TO YOU TOO, KORKY!

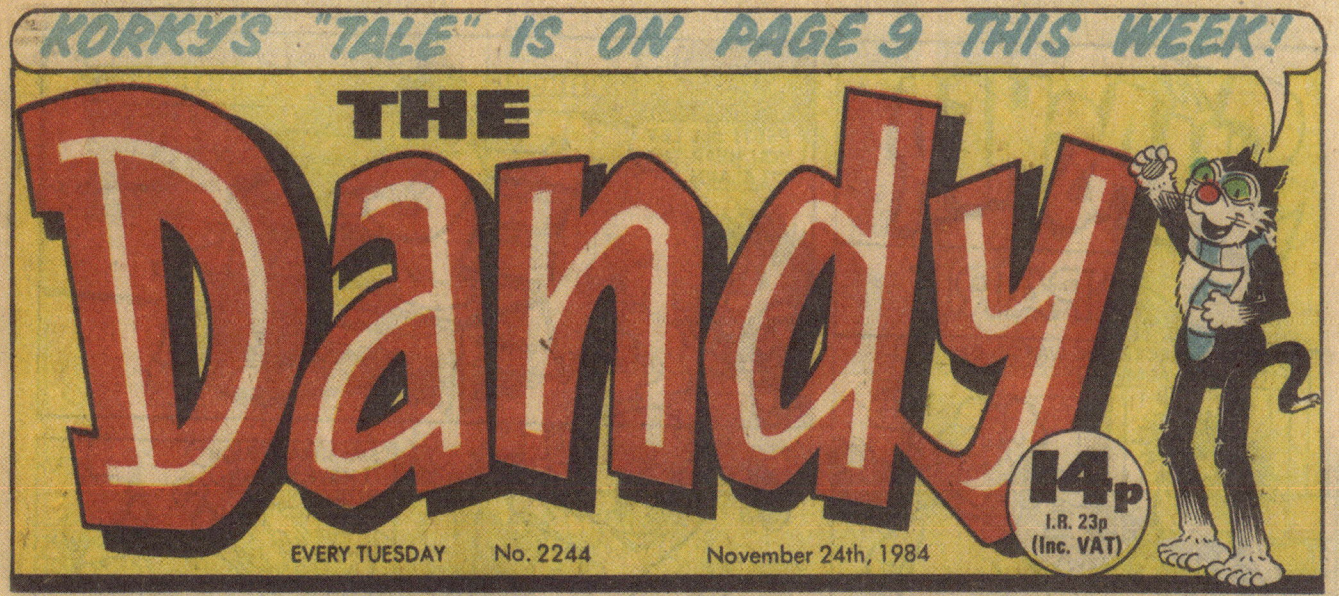

KORKY'S "TALE" IS ON PAGE 9 THIS WEEK!

# The Dandy

Every Tuesday  No. 2244  November 24th, 1984  14p  I.R. 23p (Inc. VAT)

## DESPERATE DAN

THERE'S A COMPETITION IN THE PAPER! ALL YOU HAVE TO DO IS ANSWER SOME QUESTIONS ABOUT TEXAS TO WIN A THOUSAND DOLLARS!

I'LL PACK MY BAGS, THEN GO ROUND TEXAS FINDING OUT THE ANSWERS!

NOW ALL I NEED IS MY BIKE!

HOLD IT, DAN...

...YOU CAN'T GO UNTIL YOU PUT ON THIS SIGN!

LONG VEHICLE

I LOVE TO GO A-WANDERING...

CONTINUED ON THE CENTRE PAGES

# The Dandy

**Christmas FUN FOR EVERYONE – Inside!**

EVERY TUESDAY — December 29th, 1984 — No. 2249 — 14p / I.R. 23p (Inc. VAT)

## DESPERATE DAN

"THIS IS THE TALLEST TREE AROUND! IT WILL MAKE A GREAT CHRISTMAS TREE FOR OUR TOWN!"

CHOP! "MUST BE AN ECHO AROUND HERE!"

"EH? I CAN STILL HEAR A CHOPPING SOUND!" SCRATCH! CHOP! CHOP!

"I'M CHOPPING DOWN THIS TREE FOR SMALLVILLE TOWN SQUARE, DAN!" "BUT I WANT THE TREE FOR CACTUSVILLE!"

CACTUSVILLE — DAN SORTED OUT THAT PROBLEM OF TWO TOWNS WANTING THE SAME TREE...

"...BY PULLING IT BACK AND FORTH BETWEEN HERE AND SMALLVILLE SO WE CAN SHARE THE TREE!"

HOTEL — CACTUSVILLE

**CONTINUED ON THE CENTRE PAGES**

# THE DANDY

MEET THE JOCKS AND THE GEORDIES INSIDE

*fun for boys and girls!*

EVERY TUESDAY   No. 2385   August 8th, 1987   18p I.R. 26p (Inc. VAT)

## DESPERATE DAN

"I LIKE TO GO HIKIN'!..."

SPUDS   FLOUR   COW PIE   COW PIE   VEG

"I LIKE TO GO BIKIN'!..."

STOP

"BUT EATIN' AN' DRINKIN' ARE MOST TO MAH LIKIN'!"

COW-PIE   COW-PIE   COW-PIE

OWL HOOT JUICE   OWL HOOT JUICE

CURRY POWDER EXTRA EXTRA SUPER HOT

*A WHOLE FEAST OF FUN ON THE BACK COVER—*

# THE DANDY

**Special Hallowe'en Issue**

*fun for boys and girls!*

EVERY TUESDAY   No. 2397   October 31st, 1987   20p   I.R. 29p (inc. VAT)

## DESPERATE DAN

"WONDER IF UNCLE DAN WILL HAVE A PUMPKIN LANTERN FOR HALLOWE'EN?"

FIRE MOUNTAIN (ACTIVE VOLCANO) ←

HAVE A HILARIOUS HALLOWE'EN WITH DAN ON THE BACK COVER —

# THE DANDY

**50th BIRTHDAY SPECIAL ISSUE * FREE GIANT SOUVENIR POSTER INSIDE!**

No. 2402 — December 5th, 1987 — 20p (I.R. 29p inc. VAT)

"THE DANDY'S 50 YEARS YOUNG AND YOU'RE ALL INVITED TO THE BIG PARTY INSIDE!"

Original Desperate Dan artwork for the front cover of *The Dandy* No. 2249

**Christmas FUN FOR EVERYONE—Inside!**

# The Dandy

EVERY TUESDAY — December 29th, 1984 — No. 2249

14p
I.R. 23p (Inc. VAT)

## DESPERATE DAN

**Panel 1:** THIS IS THE TALLEST TREE AROUND! IT WILL MAKE A GREAT CHRISTMAS TREE FOR OUR TOWN!

**Panel 2:** CHOP!

**Panel 3:** EH? I CAN STILL HEAR A CHOPPING SOUND! SCRATCH! CHOP! CHOP! MUST BE AN ECHO AROUND HERE!

**Panel 4:** I'M CHOPPING DOWN THIS TREE FOR SMALLVILLE TOWN SQUARE, DAN! BUT I WANT THE TREE FOR CACTUSVILLE!

**Panel 5:** CACTUSVILLE — DAN SORTED OUT THAT PROBLEM OF TWO TOWNS WANTING THE SAME TREE...

**Panel 6:** ...BY PULLING IT BACK AND FORTH BETWEEN HERE AND SMALLVILLE SO WE CAN SHARE THE TREE! CACTUSVILLE HOTEL

CONTINUED ON THE CENTRE PAGES